The Midnight Train In Georgia

By

James Soloman Smith Jr.

This book is a work of non-fiction. Names and places have been changed to protect the privacy of all individuals. The events and situations are true.

First published by AuthorHouse 05/24/04

ISBN: 1-4184-5984-4 (e-book)
ISBN: 1-4184-3236-9 (Paperback)

This book is printed on acid free paper.

DEDICATION

I, James Soloman Smith Jr., the Author of the written materials contained herein, do hereby dedicate this, my first published works, to the memory of my parents, James Soloman Smith Sr. and Betty Jane Smith, it is my prayer, that they both can observe, how I their child, have stood up for my rights! How I have actually faced the unjust way that a person can be treated by another human being, simply because of the color of their skin, not the content of their character! If I could only talk with my parents, for just one more minute, I would let them know that it was the ALL MIGHTY GOD, who they introduced me to as a small child, that brought me through this ordeal, a much better and more knowledgeable person, realizing that OUR HEAVENLY FATHER, TRULY DOES SITS HIGH AND LOOKS LOW AND THAT IF A PERSON ACTUALLY DOES KEEP THE GOD OF THEIR UNDERSTANDING IN THEIR HEARTS AS WELL AS THEIR PRAYERS, HE TRULY WILL DIRECT THEIR PATHS! JUST LIKE THEY TOLD ME THAT HE WOULD!

(JUST LIKE HE HAS DONE FOR ME)

Next, I dedicate this book, to those who are this very second, ILLEGALLY SITTING BEHIND PRISON WALLS, ALL OVER THIS COUNTRY, SIMPLY BECAUSE THEY WERE UNFORTUNATELY BORN POOR AND BLACK! I want you to know, that I FEEL YOUR PAIN! AS I TOO, HAVE EXPERIENCED FIRST HAND, WHAT IT FEELS LIKE, TO BE GUILTY, UNTIL YOU PROVE YOURSELF INNOCENT!!

Finally, I dedicate this book to my beloved family members, especially those of you who NEVER DOUBTED MY ABILITIES TO BE AN OVER/COMER OF THE INJUSTICE THAT I WAS FORCED TO ENDURE! YOU KNOW EXACTLY WHO YOU ARE! TO MY GRAND CHILDREN WHO HOPEFULLY WILL SOMEDAY READ OF THEIR GRANDFATHERS PLIGHT AND WILL STRIVE TO MAKE THIS WORLD A BETTER PLACE FOR EVERYONE!

(MAY GOD BLESS US ALL)

THE MIDNIGHT TRAIN IN GEORGIA

By

JAMES S. SMITH JR.

In my mind, I thought that I was still dreaming, but that strange annoying sound, which I was continuing to hear, never stopped! I truthfully didn't want to come out of the restful sleep, that I was enjoying, but, that Damned Annoying Sound, simply would not go away! I realized, that the only way that I was going to stop this loud and constant buzzing, was that I had to get up and see for myself, exactly what it was, that was causing this nerve-racking noise! Then, do whatever it was, that I had to do, to stop it! Anger, was the emotion which I was feeling, as I had to slowly come from the sweet restful sleep, that my body so desperately craved! I slowly opened my eyes, because, I knew that the night-lights, which were located in various places around the bedroom, was going to hurt them, the second I opened them up! I quietly wished, that I could just go back to sleep and rest, for at/least another week or two! But, that damned annoying sound, simply would not stop! No matter how hard I wished that it would! As I opened my eyes, reality suddenly snatched me by the ass! My heart started beating frantically, as I realized, that my whole family, was this very second, in extreme danger and if I didn't move and move quickly, everybody in my house, including myself, was surely going to be carried out of our lovely three bedroom home, in body bags! I quickly shook my wife Loretta, telling her of the unusual sounds that I was hearing! At that very second, I realized, that it was the sound of our smoke detector alarming! As I looked in the direction from which the noise was coming, I saw thick black smoke, slowly oozing under the base of our bedroom door! Loretta had not quite realized the seriousness of the situation, because she was still moving at her usual snail pace, which pissed me off! So, I gave her a seriously strong push, that sent her sprawling out of our bed, when she hit the bedroom floor, she actually saw the smoke that was coming under the door for herself! At that point, she realized that our house was actually on fire! She then jumped

1

to her feet in a panic mode! I knew, that I was going to have to take control of this situation! I told her to get out of the house, through the bedroom window! As she was following my instructions and heading toward the window, it apparently dawned on her, that our children were still in their bedrooms, because, she started screaming for them! I yelled at her, telling her to continue getting out of the house! I would go and get the children! She never stopped screaming their names, even though, she was doing as I had instructed her to do! Once she was out of our house safely, it dawned on me, that I was either going to get all of my family out of this now smoldering house safely, or, we were all going to come out of here in body bags, as there was no such thing as a middle of the road in a situation like this! It was all or nothing at all! I personally did not feel as if my GOD was quite ready for me at this moment, so, I quickly went about the business, of getting our four children, safely out of this smoke filled house! I also knew, from previous experience, in the United States Marine Corps, that once a building, or any enclosed structure, filled with smoke, it was just a small matter of time, before what was called a flash over, took place, igniting the dust particles in the air, erupting into super hot flames, which would more than likely, kill everybody, unlucky enough to get trapped inside! Realizing this fact, I knew, that I could not and that I would not, waste time, getting my children's clothes, shoe's, or anything else, which just might make us miss, the small window of opportunity, which I silently prayed, that we still had! As I entered my two boy's bedroom, which was directly across the hall from our bedroom, I realized that they were still sleeping, as if nothing out of the ordinary was happening! I secretly wondered, if they were simply sleeping, or had the smoke, which had slowly been filling our house, quietly lulled them, into it's deadly grasp? I didn't waste any time, I grabbed them one at a time, then, quickly shoved them through their opened bedroom window, to the out stretched arms, of their waiting mother! Who was screaming for them! As she continued screaming, I saw each of them, rubbing their eyes! Which told me, that they were only sleeping and had not been over come by the deadly smoke! Praise GOD! As they very well could have been! Once those two were out of the house safely, my attention quickly turned to my two girls, whose bedroom was just down the hall! I realized, that I had to work, as fast as I possibly could, in getting them out! Just as I turned toward their bedroom, I heard, what sounded like a Sonic Boom, which I thought came from the living room area! As I looked in that direction, I saw what appeared to be a Wall Of Flames, heading in my direction! I heard windows, as they all went shattering, out onto our porch and the ground below! Running as quickly as my short legs would allow, I made it into my daughters bedroom! Where I saw my oldest daughter, attempting to grab the youngest one, and was unsuccessful in her attempt, she wanted to take her out of the now slowly burning house, to safety! But, because of the sheer terror, which my four year old baby was engrossed in, at that very second, she was in the far corner of her bed, balled up into a tiny knot, with her knees touching her stomach, screaming and crying, in fear! I immediately snatched her out of the bed, literally throwing her through the open window, as the flames were getting closer and closer! I then instructed my oldest daughter to get the hell out of here! While she was exiting through the window, I looked around to see exactly how fast, as well as how far, the fire was moving through our house! In my heart, I knew, that it was just a small matter of time before this fire might very well, once again explode from lack of oxygen! As this fire was now gaining momentum and was rapidly spreading throughout all areas of our lovely little house! It was even burning up the little bit of oxygen, which was yet left therein! Causing me to start choking and coughing! I realized that because of this fire, we were losing a part of our family's history! I took one final and quick look around before exiting our lovely little house for the last time! To be perfectly honest with you, I actually realized that I was fighting back tears at the thought of losing our first and only piece of property that anyone in my whole family had ever acquired to this life altering fire! I also knew that I did not have the luxury of dwelling in this state of self pity, because if I didn't hurry up and get the Hell Out Of This House, all of my debts were going to be marked paid in full! As I would no longer be among the living! Moving with the quickness of a frightened ally cat, I exited through our daughters' bedroom window as the pressure from the fire once again exploded, this time shooting flames throughout our house, forcing me to the realization that my GOD really wasn't ready for me yet, because he had given me the exact amount of time that I needed to get my entire family, as well as myself, out of this inferno alive! You can be sure that I looked toward the heavens and said,

"THANK YOU LORD!"

I then took my family out to our car, which was parked a safe distance away from the fire! Putting our younger children inside, then I immediately instructed my wife and oldest daughter to go to the neighbor's house, bang on their door, yell fire, tell them to call the Fire

Department! I didn't have the time to see if they were following my orders. My oldest son and I quickly ran around to the back of our house where the garden hose was, so that we could fight the fire with this! Within approximately ten minutes, the Fire Department arrived on the scene, taking control of the situation! Approximately an hour or so after their arrival, the fire to our house had been totally extinguished! The Fire Fighters were wrapping up their hoses and putting away their equipment, when my wife and I noticed that someone had arrived in an unmarked Official State of Georgia Vehicle! As the person exited said vehicle, my wife and I saw that he was wearing a Police Badge, which was gold in color, attached to the belt that he wore around his waist! Once this Detective had fully exited his vehicle, he walked right past my wife and I without uttering one single word! He walked up to the Fire Marshall, who was doing an outside inspection of the remains of our house! Looking for hot spots! My Wife and I were standing in the grass of our front yard looking on. Reassuring each other that everything was going to be all right. We quietly observed as the Fire Marshal and the Detective finished their conversation, then, went directly into our house. Since the firefighters had finished knocking all of the remaining windows out, we did not have any problem what so ever observing every move they made while they were standing in our house, pointing and discussing various points of interest. Then the Detective came out of our house, went to the trunk of his vehicle, where he retrieved approximately twelve metal canisters, which were all wrapped together with what appeared to be some kind of masking tape. He took them back into our house, where my wife and I continued to look on in total amazement as the Fire Marshall and the Detective began to work as a team! The Fire Marshall pulled the carpet that my wife and I recently had professionally installed up from our floors, holding it up so that the Detective could use what appeared to be a large pair of sheers to cut large holes into our carpet, then putting that which they had ILLEGALLY OBTAINED FROM OUR HOUSE, INTO ONE OF THE METAL CONTAINERS! THE TWO OF THEM WENT THROUGHOUT OUR HOUSE, REPEATING THIS ACTION, OVER AND OVER AGAIN! ILLEGALLY CUTTING HOLES INTO THE CARPET ON OUR FLOORS, PUTTING THAT WHICH THEY HAD ILLEGALLY TAKEN FROM THE FLOORS OF OUR HOUSE, INTO THOSE METAL CONTAINERS!
AFTER THEY FINISHED STEALING ITEMS FROM THE FLOORING OF OUR HOUSE, MY WIFE AND I CONTINUED TO LOOK ON IN TOTAL AMAZEMENT AS

THEY WENT INTO OUR LIVING ROOM, WHERE THEY AGAIN WORKED AS A TEAM, PULLING AND CUTTING HOLES INTO OUR SOFA, THEN OUR LOVE SEAT, FINALLY THEY WENT INTO OUR DINING ROOM, WHERE WE ONCE AGAIN COULD ONLY CONTINUE LOOKING ON IN AMAZEMENT, AS THE TWO OF THEM WORKED AS A TEAM, PULLING AND CUTTING HOLES INTO THE CUSHIONS OF THE CHAIRS, WHICH WERE NEATLY SPACED AROUND OUR DINNER TABLE!

IT SHOULD BE NOTED, THAT THE ITEMS WHICH THEY TOOK FROM OUR HOUSE, WERE SUBMITTED AND WERE ACCEPTED INTO EVIDENCE AGAINST MY WIFE AND I, WHEN THIS CASE, WAS BROUGHT INTO THE SUPERIOR COURT, OF CLAYTON COUNTY GEORGIA! - The following, is exactly what the written laws state, pertaining to Officials Of The State Of Georgia, ILLEGALLY entering, searching, then presenting illegally obtained evidence into a court of law against a citizen: "A SEARCH WITHOUT A WARRANT IS PRIMA FACIE ILLEGAL AND MUST BE SHOWN TO COME WITHIN SOME RECOGNIZED EXCEPTION BEFORE THE EVIDENCE CAN BE ADMITTED".

IT MUST ALSO BE NOTED, THAT THE FIRE MARSHALL AND THE DETECTIVE ILLEGALLY SEARCHED AND SEIZED ITEMS FROM OUR HOUSE WITHOUT EITHER OF THEM, HAVING ANYTHING WHICH REMOTELY RESEMBLED A SEARCH WARRANT OF ANY KIND WHAT SO EVER! WHICH CONSTITUTES; ILLEGAL SEARCH AND SEIZURE! ACCORDING TO THE UNITED STATES CONSTITUTION! AT THIS TIME, I WANT TO INFORM YOU THE READER, AS TO EXACTLY, WHAT THE WRITTEN LAWS, WHICH ARE CURRENTLY IN THE LAW BOOKS, STATE, PERTAINING TO ANY OFFICIAL, OF THE STATE OF GEORGIA, ILLEGALLY SEARCHING A CITIZENS HOUSE WITHOUT A WARRANT; "SEARCH OF A PRIVET DWELLING WITHOUT A WARRANT IN ITSELF UNREASONABLE AND ABHORRENT TO OUR LAWS. CONGRESS HAS NEVER PASSED AN ACT PURPORTING TO AUTHORIZE THE SEARCH OF A HOUSE WITHOUT A WARRANT".

After the Detective and the Fire Marshall finished doing this to our house, my wife and I, continued to look on, as the Detective took the items which they had - (ILLEGALLY STOLEN) - FROM OUR HOUSE AND PUT THEM INTO THE TRUNK OF HIS UNMARKED POLICE VEHICLE!

The Detective then came up to my wife and I, asking us if we were the owners of this house? My wife and I both responded to his question, informing him that we were the owners, he said that his name was Detective R.T. Spiveny, Of The Clayton County Georgia Police Department. He then asked us if we knew exactly how the fire had gotten started? We both again answered him, informing him of the fact that we did not know, how the fire had gotten started. The Detective then said, "SINCE YOU TWO DON'T KNOW HOW THE FIRE GOT STARTED AND I DON'T KNOW HOW THE FIRE GOT STARTED, I AM NOW PLACING THE TWO OF YOU UNDER ARREST AND I AM CHARGING THE TWO OF YOU WITH ARSON IN THE FIRST DEGREE".

This was done to my wife and I without this Detective having one single ounce of evidence, which would, or could, point the finger of guilt at my wife or I! This Detective did not, have anyone who would, or could, say that my wife or I committed this act! This Detective did not have any proof, which could, or would, point the finger of guilt at my wife or I! He simply (ASSUMED), that we committed this act and arrested the two of us! I present exactly what the written laws state, pertaining to anyone (ASSUMING), that we broke the laws, and arresting us!! "THERE IS NO AUTHORITY UNDER WHICH A CITIZEN MAY BE ARRESTED WITHOUT A WARRANT AND HELD FOR INVESTIGATION TO DETERMINE IF HE HAS COMMITTED SOME CRIME MERELY BECAUSE THE PERSON MAKING THE ARREST HAS A SUSPICION THAT THE PERSON ARRESTED MAY HAVE COMMITTED SOME THEN UNKNOWN CRIME".

My wife and I constantly told the Arresting Detective that we would not do such a thing to our house! He did not pay us any attention at all, he acted as if what we were saying did not matter to him! He even made my wife and I set and watch as the child protection workers arrived and took our children away! Putting them into the foster care programs administered by the State of Georgia!

I present the fact, that this Detective on THE CLAYTON COUNTY GEORGIA POLICE DEPARTMENT, WHO WAS A FOURTEEN YEAR VETERAN DETECTIVE AT THIS

POINT, CERTAINLY KNEW OF WHAT THE WRITTEN LAWS WERE PERTAINING TO THE CHARGE OF ARSON IN THE FIRST DEGREE! WHICH ARE AS FOLLOWS: "Only the dwelling house of another can be the subject of arson, but occupancy, rather than ownership is the test, thus a landlord can be guilty of arson by burning the dwelling house of his tenant, but the tenant or occupant cannot be guilty of arson by burning his own dwelling house".

(legal citations can and will be issued upon written request) ———— Therefore, ACCORDING TO THE WRITTEN LAWS, my wife or I, have never broken any kind of law, what so ever! Yet we were both thrown into THE CLAYTON COUNTY GEORGIA DETENTION FACILITY!

(THE COUNTY JAIL)

Once we were locked into this facility, after approximately three weeks of being illegally arrested, under severe stress, along with serious worry for my children, my wife, my house and not knowing what was going to come of this railroading of my wife and I into this situation, that we now found ourselves in. I woke up one morning and saw every single strain of hair that was on my body, had simply fallen off of my body and was lying on my bed! My wife and I were made to simply set in this jail and just wait, we were NOT, taken into any kind of Court Of Law, for (52) fifty-two days! The arresting Detective told us, as he was finishing his paperwork, which would actually confine us into this facility, "Unless one of you, or both of you, admit to setting your house on fire, you both can rot in here for all I care." We NEVER had a first appearance hearing! Yet, the written laws states; "IMMEDIATELY FOLLOWING ANY ARREST, BUT NO LATER THAN 48 HOURS, IF THE ARREST WAS WITHOUT A WARRANT, OR 72 HOURS FOLLOWING AN ARREST WITH A WARRANT, UNLESS THE ACCUSED HAD MADE BOND IN THE MEANTIME, THE ARRESTING OFFICER OR THE OFFICER HAVING CUSTODY OF THE ACCUSED SHALL PRESENT THE ACCUSED IN PERSON BEFORE A MAGISTRATE OR OTHER JUDICIAL OFFICER FOR FIRST APPEARANCE".
(LEGAL CITATIONS CAN AND WILL BE ISSUED UPON REQUEST)

On the fifty-second day of being illegally imprisoned, my wife and I were taken into our very first court of law! We both had filled out the necessary forms, which were supposed to have gotten an attorney assigned to represent us! However, when we were taken into said court, we did not have any kind of legal representation, of any kind, what so ever! All questions which were asked of our accusers, were asked by me! Also, the only persons that were in this court to testify against my wife and I were the Arresting Detective and The Fire Marshall, of which, neither one of these two men were anywhere near our house before the fire occurred, that we knew of, therefore, their testimony's should not have been admitted into court against my wife and I! However, my wife and I were bound over to stand trial, in:

The Superior Court of Clayton County Georgia!

After this hearing was over, when my wife and I were taken back to The Clayton County Georgia Detention Facility, there were two (2) undercover informants put into the same area and the same cell that I was being detained in! With apparent instructions to get some kind of incriminating information on me! The informant that was assigned to the cell with me would sit on the floor when the lights were turned off, listening to hear if I was going to say something incriminating while I was sleeping! On several occasions, I woke up having to use the bathroom, to find this person jumping away from my face in his attempts to hear if I was going to possibly say something incriminating! After approximately three weeks of their failed attempts, they were simply taken away! Shortly thereafter, I received my copy of the Grand Jury Issued Indictment. As I looked it over, I realized that the undercover informants had actually told LIES, to those who had sent them into the detention area! Also, the one's who they told the lies to, apparently went to the Grand Jury with those lies, causing them to issue a second charge of Solicitation to Commit, onto the indictment!

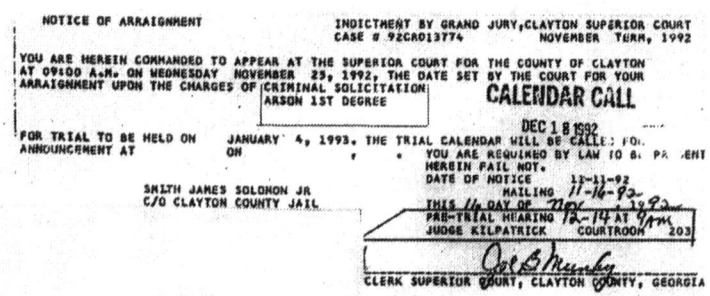

By the time I received my copy of the indictment, I had been confined in THE CLAYTON COUNTY GEORGIA DETENTION FACILITY, for almost six months, during which time, I saw many, many, inmates who had obtained a second charge while they were confined herein! Each and every one of them had been taken to the intake area of the Detention Facility, where they were informed of the newly acquired charge! Then, they were re-finger printed pertaining to the newly acquired charge! Next, they had their pictures again taken and attached to the Detention Facility's files, for identification purposes, pertaining to the newly acquired charge! Also they had their MIRANDA RIGHTS READ TO THEM PERTAINING TO THIS NEWLY ACQUIRED CHARGE! FINALLY THEY WERE ALL

ISSUED A COPY OF THE NEWLY ACQUIRED CHARGE BY THE PEOPLE WHO HELD THEM IN CUSTODY! AS THIS IS THE STANDARD OPERATING PROCEDURE, AS WELL AS THE LAW! YET NONE OF THIS HAS EVER OCCURRED PERTAINING TO MY CASE! YET I HAD THIS NEW CHARGE ISSUED AGAINST ME ON MY INDICTMENT, WHICH HAD BEEN HANDED DOWN BY THE GRAND JURY! THIS MAKES THE INDICTMENT AUTOMATICALLY BECOME A FRAUDULENT DOCUMENT! AS IT CANNOT POSSIBLY BE A TRUE BILL, AS INDICATED ON ITS FACE! AND A LIE AT THE SAME TIME! Shortly after receiving my copy of the indictment, this case was brought into the Superior Court of Clayton County Georgia for the actual trial to take place. When I was brought into the courtroom the presiding Judge called the court to order, then informed the whole court of the fact that UNDER NO CIRCUMSTANCES WAS HE, OR THE STATE OF GEORGIA, GOING TO ASSIGN ME AN ATTORNEY TO REPRESENT ME, PERTAINING TO THE CHARGES WHICH I HAVE BEEN INDICTED FOR! ANY DEFENSE THAT WAS GOING TO BE PRESENTED ON MY BEHALF WOULD HAVE TO COME FROM ME! FORCING ME INTO SELF-REPRESENTATION OF A JURY TRIAL, WHICH LASTED FOR TWO WEEKS! I HAD ABSOLUTELY NO LEGAL HELP WHAT SO EVER, PERTAINING TO THIS TRIAL! THEN THE PRESIDING JUDGE TURNED AROUND AND IMMEDIATELY ASSIGNED MY WIFE THE SERVICES OF AN ATTORNEY TO REPRESENT HER THROUGHOUT EVERY PHASE OF THIS JURY TRIAL! IT SHOULD BE NOTED, THAT I HAVE NEVER EVEN BEEN INSIDE THE CORRIDORS OF ANY KIND OF LAW SCHOOL IN MY LIFE! WHICH MAKES THIS WHOLE PROCEEDING AGAINST THE LAW!

IT IS IN DIRECT VIOLATION OF THE FOURTEENTH AMENDMENT OF THE CONSTITUTION OF THE UNITED STATES! AS FAILURE TO ASSIGN ME COURT APPOINTED COUNSEL, VIOLATES DUE PROCESS OF LAW! ALONG WITH SEVERAL OTHER CONSTITUTIONAL AMENDMENTS! THE PRESIDING JUDGE MADE ME DO THE SELECTING OF THE PERSPECTIVE JURORS, EXAMINE, AS WELL AS CROSS EXAMINE THEM! HE FORCED ME INTO QUESTIONING THEIR MOTIVES, AS TO WHY THEY WOULD MAKE AN IMPARTIAL PERSPECTIVE JUROR, THEN, HE FORCED ME INTO SELECTING THOSE THAT WOULD MAKE

THE BEST QUALIFIED CANDIDATES! ELIMINATING THE OTHERS! I HAD NO IDEA WHAT SO EVER AS TO WHAT I WAS BEING FORCED INTO DOING BY THE PRESIDING JUDGE! BUT, I REALIZED THAT IF I DIDN'T, AT THE VERY LEAST, ATTEMPT TO FOLLOW HIS INSTRUCTIONS, THIS WOULD MAKE THE PRESIDING JUDGE ANGRY, AND WHO KNOWS WHAT HE COULD HAVE SAID, OR DONE TO MY WIFE AND I? HIS ATTITUDE CLEARLY TOLD ME THAT HE WAS GOING TO SEND ME TO PRISON BY ANY MEANS POSSIBLE! HIS ATTITUDE ALSO MADE HIS DISLIKE FOR ME CLEARLY KNOWN! HOWEVER, I REALIZED THAT IF I COOPERATED WITH HIM, THE VIOLATIONS, WHICH THE PRESIDING JUDGE WAS PERPETRATING AGAINST ME, WOULD BE A PART OF THE RECORD! SO I FOLLOWED HIS ORDERS, DOING EVERYTHING THAT THE PRESIDING JUDGE TOLD ME TO DO! TO THE VERY BEST OF MY ABILITY! ONCE THE JURY MEMBERS WERE ALL SELECTED AND SEATED, THE PRESIDING JUDGE CALLED ME UP TO HIS DESK, THEN HE SAID TO ME IN A LOUD AND CLEAR VOICE SO THAT EVERYONE IN THE COURTROOM COULD HEAR EXACTLY WHAT HE WAS SAYING, AS HE SAID, "MR. SMITH, YOU ARE THIS DAY, BEING CHARGED WITH TWO SEPARATE FELONIES, YOU ARE BEING CHARGED WITH;

COUNT #1.) ARSON IN THE FIRST DEGREE.

AND COUNT #2.) SOLICITATION TO COMMIT.

MR. SMITH, THESE ARE VERY SERIOUS CHARGES, WHICH ARE BEING PRESENTED AGAINST YOU! THE GRAND JURY HAS HANDED DOWN THESE CHARGES, AGAINST YOU AND ONCE THE GRAND JURY HANDS DOWN CHARGES AGAINST AN INDIVIDUAL, IT IS TOTALLY OUT OF THIS COURTS HANDS, AS THE CHARGES CANNOT BE ALTERED IN ANY MANNER WHAT SO EVER BY LAW! THIS COURT IS POWERLESS TO ALTER THESE CHARGES, THE DISTRICT ATTORNEY IS POWERLESS TO ALTER THESE CHARGES, AND CERTAINLY YOU MR. SMITH, ARE POWERLESS TO ALTER THESE CHARGES! THEREFORE, THIS COURT WANTS YOU TO SPEAK UP, IN A LOUD AND CLEAR VOICE WHEN YOU ANSWER THIS QUESTION, WHICH IS: EXACTLY HOW DO

YOU INTEND TO PLEA TO THESE CHARGES, WHICH HAVE BEEN PRESENTED AGAINST YOU, MR. SMITH".

AT THIS POINT, I CLEARED MY THROAT, SO THAT WHEN I SPOKE, THE WHOLE COURT WOULD HEAR ME AS I TOLD THE PRESIDING JUDGE OF THE FACT THAT, "I HAVE NEVER HEARD OF THE CHARGE OF SOLICITATION TO COMMIT BEFORE IN MY LIFE! I HAVE NEVER BEEN FINGER PRINTED PERTAINING TO THIS CHARGE! I HAVE NEVER BEEN ISSUED A COPY OF THIS CHARGE, BY THOSE WHO WERE HOLDING ME IN CONFINEMENT! I HAVE NEVER BEEN TO THE INTAKE AREA OF THE DETENTION FACILITY AND INFORMED OF SAID NEW CHARGE! I HAVE NEVER HAD MY MIRANDA RIGHTS READ TO ME, BY THOSE WHO WERE HOLDING ME IN CUSTODY! PERTAINING TO THIS SOLICITATION TO COMMIT CHARGE! IN FACT, THE ONLY WAY THAT I HEARD OF THIS CHARGE, WAS WHEN I READ ABOUT IT, ONCE I RECEIVED MY COPY OF THE INDICTMENT, WHICH WAS ONLY THREE DAYS BEFORE THIS CASE WAS BROUGHT INTO THIS COURTROOM".

THE PRESIDING JUDGE IMMEDIATELY JUMPED UP FROM HIS DESK, SNATCHED OFF HIS GLASSES, STARED AT ME IN A VERY THREATENING MANNER, THEN WALKED OUT OF THE COURTROOM! APPARENTLY HE WENT AND CHECKED OUT THAT WHICH I INFORMED HIM OF, MAKING SURE THAT WHAT I HAD SAID WAS THE TRUTH. BECAUSE WHEN HE RETURNED TO THE COURTROOM, THE PRESIDING JUDGE SPLIT THE CHARGING TERMS OF THE INDICTMENT IN HALF! NOW, ONLY CHARGING ME WITH THE CHARGE OF ARSON IN THE FIRST DEGREE! TOTALLY ALTERING THE INDICTMENT! THIS WAS MUCH, MUCH, AFTER THE INDICTMENT HAD BEEN RETURNED FROM THE GRAND JURY, YET, HE HAD JUST RECENTLY TOLD ME AND THE WHOLE COURT THAT NO ONE COULD ALTER AN INDICTMENT ONCE IT HAD BEEN RETURNED FROM THE GRAND JURY! THE FOLLOWING IS EXACTLY WHAT THE WRITTEN LAWS STATES PERTAINING TO ANYONE ALTERING AN INDICTMENT, AFTER IT HAS BEEN RETURNED FROM THE GRAND JURY: - - - "BECAUSE THE 5TH AMENDMENT GUARANTEE'S A DEFENDANT THE RIGHT TO BE TRIED ONLY ON THOSE OFFENSES PRESENTED IN AN INDICTMENT

RETURNED BY A GRAND JURY, A SUBSTANTIVE AMENDMENT IS REVERSIBLE ERROR, SUCH AN AMENDMENT OCCURS, WHEN THE PROSECUTION OR THE COURT EITHER LITERALLY, OR CONSTRUCTIVELY, ALTERS THE CHARGING TERMS OF AN INDICTMENT, AFTER IT HAS BEEN RETURNED BY A GRAND JURY". - - THE PRESIDING JUDGE MADE SURE THAT ONCE I WAS (ILLEGALLY) FOUND TO BE GUILTY FOR THE CHARGE OF ARSON IN THE FIRST DEGREE, HE WAS ABLE TO SENTENCE ME! USING A FRAUDULENT INDICTMENT IN DOING SO! SENTENCING ME TO A SEVEN-YEAR TERM IN THE STATE PRISON SYSTEM! YET, THE WRITTEN LAW STATES THAT MY WIFE AND I HAD NOT BROKEN ANY KIND OF LAW WHAT SO EVER, EVEN IF WE DID SET OUR HOUSE, OUR HOME, OUR PLACE OF DWELLING, ON FIRE! WHICH WE DID NOT DO! THEREFORE, HOW COULD I POSSIBLY BE FOUND TO BE GUILTY? FOR THE CRIME OF ARSON IN THE FIRST DEGREE? WHEN NO LAW WAS EVER BROKEN? AS THE CRIME OF ARSON WAS NEVER COMMITTED BY ANYONE IN MY FAMILY? ACCORDING TO THE WRITTEN LAWS, WHICH ARE CURRENTLY ON THE LAW BOOKS? THIS CONSTITUTES RAILROADING OF ME INTO THE PRISON SYSTEM! BEFORE I LEFT THE COURTROOM, BEFORE THE TRIAL HAD ENDED, I MADE SURE THAT I INFORMED THE COURT OF THE FACT THAT I WANTED TO APPEAL THIS RENDERED DECISION! ALSO, THAT I WANTED TO BE ASSIGNED AN ATTORNEY FOR APPEAL PURPOSES! ONCE I ARRIVED AT THE JACKSON GEORGIA INTAKE PRISON, WHERE I WAS GOING TO BE STAYING FOR THE NEXT SIX TO TWELVE WEEKS,

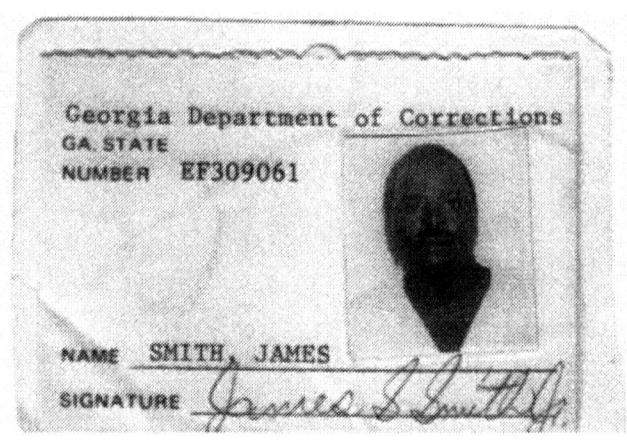

I SENT THE SENTENCING COURT A SIGNED, DATED, NOTARIZED MOTION, ONCE AGAIN, REQUESTING THAT I GET AN ATTORNEY ASSIGNED TO MY CASE, FOR APPEAL PURPOSES, INFORMING THE COURT OF THE FACT THAT I AM AN INDIGENT STATE INMATE AND THAT ACCORDING TO THE UNITED STATES CONSTITUTION, I AM SUPPOSED TO GET AN ATTORNEY ASSIGNED TO REPRESENT ME ON MY INITIAL APPEAL AS OF RIGHT! I ALSO FILED A MOTION REQUESTING THAT I GET A COPY OF THE TRANSCRIPT OF THE CASE ONCE AGAIN STATING THAT THIS TOO WAS ONE OF THE CONSTITUTIONALLY PROTECTED RIGHTS AND THAT I WAS SUPPOSED TO GET SAID TRANSCRIPT AT THE PUBLIC'S EXPENSE! THE PRESIDING JUDGE SENT ME HIS SIGNED DATED RESPONSE, WHICH STATED THAT THE REQUEST FOR THE APPOINTMENT OF AN ATTORNEY AND THE REQUEST FOR A COPY OF THE TRANSCRIPT WERE DENIED!

THIS JUDGE HAS A TOTAL DISREGARD FOR THE CONSTITUTION OF THE UNITED STATES OF AMERICA, BECAUSE HE NOT ONLY VIOLATED MOST OF MY CIVIL, HUMAN AND CONSTITUTIONAL RIGHTS, WHEN MY CASE WAS BEFORE HIM, HE ALSO CONTINUED VIOLATING MY CIVIL, HUMAN AND CONSTITUTIONAL RIGHTS AFTER HE HAD ILLEGALLY RAILROADED ME INTO THE PRISON SYSTEM! THEN HE TURNS AROUND AND OPENLY PUT SAID VIOLATIONS INTO WRITING WITH HIS DATED AND WRITTEN SIGNATURE CLEARLY AFFIXED THERE UNTO! AS THE FOLLOWING PAGE SHOWS THE PRESIDING JUDE IS DIRECTLY AND OPENLY VIOLATING THE FOURTEENTH AMENDMENT OF THE CONSTITUTION, WHICH IS DUE PROCESS OF LAW! ALONG WITH MANY OTHER CIVIL, HUMAN AND CONSTITUTIONAL VIOLATIONS!

IN THE SUPERIOR COURT OF CLAYTON COUNTY

- STATE OF GEORGIA

STATE OF GEORGIA)   CASE NO. 92-CR-01377-4
)
    vs.   )
)
JAMES SOLOMON SMITH, JR.,)
    Defendant.   )

ORDER OF COURT

On March 22, 1993, defendant filed a Motion For The
Appointment of Counsel, and a Motion To Produce Records
and Transcripts.   The motions are denied.

THIS the ___2___ day of July, 1993.

KENNETH KILPATRICK
Judge, Superior Court
Clayton Judicial Circuit

It goes without saying, that I was denied any kind of relief from this illegal arrest, illegal prosecution and this illegal imprisonment, when this case was presented to the GEORGIA STATE COURT OF APPEALS! I WAS INFORMED THAT THERE WAS NO WAY THAT I WAS GOING TO GET AN ATTORNEY ASSIGNED TO REPRESENT ME ON APPEAL OF THIS CONVICTION! ALSO, I WAS IN CUSTODY OF THE GEORGIA STATE PRISON SYSTEM! (I WAS NOT), ALLOWED TO GO INTO THE GEORGIA STATE COURT OF APPEALS SO THAT I COULD GIVE MY TESTIMONY PERTAINING TO THIS CASE! WHEN THE ACTUAL TRIAL WAS ON GOING, (I DID NOT) HAVE ANYONE IN THIS COURT WHO WOULD REPRESENT ME, OR MY CONCERNS, THEREFORE IT WAS UTTERLY IMPOSSIBLE FOR ME TO WIN A FAVORABLE JUDGMENT, WHICH WOULD OVERTURN THIS ILLEGAL CONVICTION!

Court of Appeals of Georgia
Room 617 State Judicial Building
MARION T. POPE, JR.
CHIEF JUDGE
ATLANTA, APRIL, 199·

Attention of all counsel is directed to Rule 2 of the Court of Appeals of Georgia.

The following cases have been placed on the calendar for argument pursuant to request in accordance with Rule 8(a). Generally, the cases will be called in the order listed and on the days named, beginning at 10 o'clock a.m. As an accommodation to the bar and pro se parties, the Court will call cases out of turn in which counsel or pro se parties respectively inform the Clerk that time of argument will be limited to 5 minutes per side or 10 minutes per side, pursuant to Rule 8(f).

TUESDAY, APRIL 05, 1994
SECOND DIVISION–A. W. BIRDSONG, JR., PRESIDING JUDGE
G. ALAN BLACKBURN, CLARENCE COOPER, JUDGES

A94A0916	TOMMY M. KIDD V. WILLIAM UNGER EXECUTOR OF THE ESTATE OF LENA A. KIDD	A94A0977	DAVID MCMILLAN ET AL V. CARROLL E. GAY, JR. ET AL
A94A0913	CECIL E. MCHAFFIE V. DECATUR FEDERAL SAVINGS AND LOAN ASSOCIATION ET AL	A94A0983	W. R. ROYSTER V. DAVID H. TISINGER
A94A0933	JAMES S. SMITH, JR. V. THE STATE	A94A0984	W. R. ROYSTER V. DAVID H. TISINGER
A94A0935	NORTHBROOK PROPERTY AND CASUALTY INSURANCE COMPANY V. CRITERION CASUALTY COMPANY	A94A0987	MITCHELL SIMPSON, SR. V. THE STATE
		A94A1000	EDWARD SIMS V. THE STATE
		A94A1008	JOYCE FINCH ET AL V. NEAL L. WEAVER
A94A0949	VAN O. DAVIS ET AL V. ROGER D. KITTLE ET AL	A94A1011	JOSEPH BERNARD HOLLAND V. THE STATE
A94A0953	DEBORAH CARSWELL ET AL V. MIDDLE GEORGIA POOLS ET AL	A93A2412	WALTER BROWN V. FRANKLIN COUNTY ET AL

WEDNESDAY, APRIL 06, 1994
SECOND DIVISION–A. W. BIRDSONG, JR., PRESIDING JUDGE
G. ALAN BLACKBURN, CLARENCE COOPER, JUDGES

A94A1047	GENE S. TRUCANO V. CHARLES M. ROSENBERG, D.D.S.	A94A1127	PATRICIA JOHNSON V. GWINNETT COUNTY ET AL
A94A1048	SUPER DISCOUNT MARKETS, INC. D/B/A CUB FOODS V. MINNI FAY CLARK	A94A1134	MIDLAND MECHANICAL CONTRACTORS, INC. V. STEPHENSON ASSOCIATES, INC.
A94A1050	DICIE LYKINS ET AL V. NATIONWIDE MUTUAL INSURANCE COMPANY ET AL	A94A1139	IN RE: BENTLEY C. ADAMS, III
A94A1051	DICIE LYKINS V. NATIONWIDE MUTUAL INSURANCE COMPANY ET AL	A94A1146	JOSEPH ALAN JACKSON ET AL V. BEECH AIRCRAFT CORPORATION
A94A1052	C. W. MATTHEWS CONTRACTING COMPANY, INC. V. MARCUS E. COLLINS, SR. ET AL	A94A1147	BEECH AIRCRAFT CORPORATION V. JOSEPH ALAN JACKSON ET AL
A94A1108	A. DERRELL HIGHTOWER V. CENTURY 21 PARISH REALTY	A94A1148	BEECH AIRCRAFT CORPORATION V. JOSEPH ALAN JACKSON ET AL
A94A1113	THE STATE V. RICHARD MONROE JONES	A94A1154	FRANK L. BROWN V. CITY OF MARIETTA
		A94A1156	BRUCE TURRY ET AL V. HONG KONG DELIGHT, INC.

TUESDAY, APRIL 12, 1994
FIRST DIVISION–MARION T. POPE, JR., CHIEF JUDGE
WILLIAM LeROY McMURRAY, JR., PRESIDING JUDGE, J. D. SMITH, JUDGE

A94A0906	SOUTHEAST REDUCING COMPANY, INC. ET AL V. NORMAN WASSERMAN	A94A0978	LOYD E. HORTON ET AL V. S. BOYD EATON, JR., M.D.
A94A0909	ROBERT F. THOMPSON, JR. ET AL V. TRUST COMPANY BANK OF MIDDLE GEORGIA, N.A. ET AL	A94A0996	TMS INSURANCE AGENCY, INC. V. JEFFERY L. HERSH ET AL
A94A0914	SOUTHERN MUTUAL INSURANCE COMPANY V. NICHOLAS OLIVER B/N/F OLLIE K. OLIVER ET AL	A94A1013	JACQUELINE C. MORSE ET AL V. FLINT RIVER COMMUNITY HOSPITAL ET AL
A94A0924	RODNEY NICHOLAS MCGUGAN V. THE STATE	A94A1014	FLINT RIVER COMMUNITY HOSPITAL ET AL V. JACQUELINE C. MORSE ET AL
A94A0946	PAMELA MARTIN ROSS V. THE STATE	A94A1015	RAJ GUPTA, M.D. V. JACQUELINE C. MORSE ET AL
A94A0942	DEBORAH MCCURLEY ET AL V. CAROLE LUDWIG	A94A1023	TRACY L. CHEEVERS V. FREDERICK L. CLARK
A94A0948	BARBARA CRAIG V. RED LOBSTER RESTAURANT ET AL	A94A1038	HUDGINS & COMPANY, INC. V. J & M TANK LINES, INC.
A94A0962	R. T. PATTERSON FUNERAL HOME, INC. ET AL V. WILLIAM H. HEAD	A94A0947	CARING HANDS, INC. V. GEORGIA DEPARTMENT OF HUMAN RESOURCES
A94A0972	DAVID H. DICK ET AL V. NEAL L. WILLIAMS ET AL		

January 14, 1994

NOTICE TO COUNSEL AND PRO SE PARTIES

All Counsel and Pro Se Parties who wish oral argument must check in with the Clerk at 9:30 AM in the Court of Appeals Court Room on the 6th Floor of the Judicial Building on the day oral argument is scheduled.

Counsel and Pro Se Parties should announce their names to the Clerk and indicate whether they wish 5, 10 or 15 minute oral argument. If Counsel and Pro Se Parties do not agree on length of oral argument, the longer time shall control.

Your cooperation and timely reporting to the Clerk will greatly assist the Court in its effort to begin promptly at 10:00 AM.

Thank you for your anticipated cooperation.

Sincerely,

William L. Martin, III
Clerk and Court Administrator
Court of Appeals of Georgia

WLM, III/sc

18

After (I was denied) the opportunity to go into court to present my side of the testimony to the GEORGIA STATE COURT OF APPEALS, by those that were holding me in custody, I shortly thereafter received a letter from the Georgia State Appellate Court informing me of the fact that my appeal had been denied, and the conviction which had been rendered against me in the Superior Court of Clayton County Georgia, was to stand as it is! It should be noted that all while I was confined in the GEORGIA STATE PRISON SYSTEM, under illegal conditions, and I personally knew that this was the case! I did not have any desire what so ever to partake of any of the activities in which the other inmates were enjoying! My one and only goal was to get the hell out of this, the prison system, legally! It was during this time that I went to the bathroom one day and noticed that when I had a bowel movement, my stool had turned Jet Black! I reported this to the medical staff, who sent me to the prisoners hospital, they informed me of the fact that I was now suffering with Bleeding Ulcers! Then told me that I needed surgery! I told them that under no conditions would I authorize them to do any kind of surgery on me! They gave me some pills and sent me back to the prison from which I had came! While the other inmates were busy lifting weights, playing basketball, writing letters and other such things, I personally spent every second that I was allowed to spend inside of the law library! Researching the various laws as they pertained to my particular case. The more that I studied, the more I became knowledgeable of various other violations, which had taken place pertaining to this case. For example, I discovered that I was being forced into INVOLUNTARY SERVITUDE, which is against the thirteenth amendment to THE UNITED STATES CONSTITUTION. I saw where I had the constitutionally protected right, even as a convicted state inmate, to file a HABEAS CORPUS PETITION WITH THE UNITED STATES FEDERAL DISTRICT COURTS, once my one and only appeal had been denied! Or, I could appeal these violations, which had taken place pertaining to this case, up to the GEORGIA STATE SUPREME COURT. The ultimate decision was totally up to me! Realizing that I had not gotten anything which resembled justice, or a fair trial, in the GEORGIA STATE COURTS, I decided to file my HABEAS CORPUS PETITION with the UNITED STATES FEDERAL DISTRICT COURTS FOR THE NORTHERN DISTRICT OF GEORGIA THE NINTH CIRCUIT! Therefore, I decided to double-check all of the violations which I was going to submit to this court! Making sure that every single law, which I presented and stated, had been violated, was the truth, accurate and could withstand any and all investigations! The more time that I spent as I sheppardized the written laws, the more comfortable I became with the study of laws! With this newly acquired knowledge of the laws, which I had obtained by constantly studying laws as they pertained to my case! I felt it was my duty to be some kind of assistance to my fellow inmates, because in the short amount of time, which I was confined in prison, I saw, as well as heard, about many, many people who had been as I had been, which was railroaded into this prison system! I also made sure, that I listened to what the inmates were saying. Responding to any and all questions presented to me by any and all of my fellow inmates! Being extremely careful to never intentionally present the image that I was better, or smarter than they were! Simply because I was not! You can be damned sure that if a person were to make one of these inmates that were locked into the institution in which I was presently being confined in, located in Macon Georgia, feel as if they were for any reason not your equal, or that you though that you were for some reason better that they were, you very well just might find yourself with your throat cut wide open! The very least thing that you could damned well be very sure of was that you were going to have to fight your ass off on an extremely regular basis! Therefore, you or anyone that might befriend you, were going to live a very uncomfortable lifestyle while you were doing your time! To make sure that this was not going to be the kind of problem which I was going to have to deal with, I stopped everything that I was working on, every day, then I would listen to the complaints of my fellow inmates, which you can be sure, that every person in this prison had, including me! I discovered, that what we all actually really wanted was to simply talk over our complaints and problems with someone who would listen and possibly have a kind word in response! One day, an inmate came to me who could not read or write his name, even if his very life depended on it! He had tears softly dripping from his eyes, he asked me, could he talk to me? I told him to have a seat on my bunk bed. He was very hesitant about doing this, because there are a few unwritten laws that exist in any and all prison institutions, one of them is if an inmate is found sitting on another inmates bunk bed, he is either his bitch, waiting for her man to come home, or he is letting the inmate whose bed that he is sitting on know that he has nothing but total disrespect for him and wants to fight at the earliest opportunity! Which usually ended up with the inmate that was sitting on the bed, getting his head split wide open, down to the white meat! When a person is doing

20

prison time, especially in the State of Georgia, they had better first of all, come into the prison system with their mouths closed and their eyes wide open! Listening to and learning of the way that the prison, which they are assigned, operates! As the people that are surrounding you on a daily basis are the one's who are the killers, murderers, dope sellers, along with every other kind of scum that walked freely on the streets of Georgia for a brief while! However, there were also people who were locked into the system like several of the people that I had the sheer pleasure of meeting, such as the inmate who I was talking about earlier, named Robert Anderson! This man grew up on a farm outside of the township of Jessup Georgia, he never had the opportunity to attend any kind of school! The closest school to the farm in which he grew up on, was more than twenty-five miles away! Therefore, he couldn't read or write his name, even if his life depended on it! However, he knew that he had been wrongfully arrested, wrongfully prosecuted and wrongfully sent to prison! He was one of the few people that treated me in a kind manner when I first arrived at this prison! I kind of took a special liking to him, even though there was absolutely no way that I was going to be able to let this be known! When I would finish my work detail for the day, I then would take my shower, change my clothes, so that I could go and research the various laws in the law library pertaining to my particular case. I would always see him carefully and quietly watching my every move! At one time I started to step to him and question why he was checking me out so hard, but I decided against doing that! As he was a member of the Country Boy's Crew! In this prison, those were the inmates who actually ran it! As time went by, several of the inmates slowly started seeking my advice, asking various kinds of legal questions! Since they constantly saw me going to the law library! I would do the best that I could to actually give them a truthful answer to their questions! If I couldn't answer them that particular day, I would surely be able to bring them an answer the very next day at the very latest! Some of the answers to the questions that they asked me would be the kind that they wanted to hear, which would bring a smile to their faces, while some of the responses that I would bring back to them, would be the kind that they would simply hate! I made sure that they would understand this before I would allow them to tell me about their situations! However, this inmate named Robert Anderson, who I recently spoke of, simply kept his mouth closed, continuing to just look on! One day the Correctional Officers came and got him, taking him toward the warden's office. From what was being said on the prison grape wine, he was being told that his mother had passed away from having a severe bout with cancer! They were taking him to her services, which was a three-day taste of freedom! Personally, I would not want to get just a taste of freedom if I couldn't have it everyday! But given his situation, it was understandable that he had to go! As this was the very last time that he was ever going to see his mother on this planet ever again! When he returned, he came straight up to me, asking me to please allow him to talk with me for a while! Since this was a Sunday, the law library was closed. I told him to come to my bunk after we had dinner! Just like clock work, as soon as dinner was over, he was waiting, as I had expected! I came up and took my usual seat on the edge of my bunk bed, the side that was closest to my locker, in the event that he told me something, which may have caused me to go therein, such as, writing material, or legal material, which I kept copied and stocked inside! As this man began to tell me of his tragic situation, I personally found it hard to believe! He told me of how his mother and father had come down with cancer, his father had it in the lungs, while his mother had it in her throat! They both were taking some kind of strong medications, which helped them be able to get around and simply exist. His parents realized that they were both simply hanging on, waiting for the end to come! Since they were too weak to do so, they asked him to take one of their 6 cows to the butchers, have him to cut the cow up, then take the freshly cut meat to one of the neighbors house, who would give him money for the meat, then he was to take the money and get some more of the medicine, bring it back home, then go and pay the butcher! Just as he was walking down the road with the cow in tow, one of the white people who lived in the area, saw a black man pulling a cow, got on their cell phone and called the police, who came out to check. Finding this black man pulling this cow, they immediately assumed that he had stolen the cow! Arresting him, prosecuted him convicted him, then sent him to prison for ten (10) years! I just knew that he was telling me a damned lie! So I told him that I was going to get the necessary papers, which we could fill out, so that he could get a copy of the transcript of the case! Thinking that this would make him say something like, that's all right, or never mind! Which was the way that most of the inmates would respond to me, when I would catch them in a lie! However, this man, Robert Anderson, never backed down when I put him to my test! The next morning he once again asked me was I still going to do that for him? I continued thinking that this man was telling me a damned lie, as I truly did not want to

22

believe anyone could, or would, treat another human being the way that this man told me he had been treated! However, I had my reputation to keep! Also, I realized, that he was damned sure going to tell his crew members of the fact that I had said that I was going to help him! So I was more or less trapped into helping this man! Who in my heart, I knew that he had to be telling me one of the biggest damned lies that I had heard, in a long time! However, I had to do as I said I was going to do! Because, one of the main violations that an inmate could possibly make was to tell another inmate a damn lie! In prison, this was one of the violations, which was punishable by death! The kind that you didn't know who, where, or even when it was coming! I therefore, kept my word, by getting, filling out and mailing the necessary papers, to the sentencing court for him! Requesting that they send him a copy of the transcript of his case! After I had done this for him, many of his so called home/boys from the area of Georgia that he came from, were not only accepting of me, they welcomed me, into their area of the prison with open arms! Realizing that they were looking out for my back, I was once again able to get back into my groove of researching the laws, taking notes, and answering legal questions, for any and all of the inmates that accepted and trusted me! While I was also keeping my noise clean! One day, approximately two months later, Robert came running up to me smiling with a large envelope in his hands, telling me that they had sent him this mail, asking me to read it and tell him what it was all about! As I opened it and read it, I realized that this man was not telling me a lie at all, in fact, everything that he had said, pertaining to his case, was more or less, written down in this paperwork, in black and white! As I read over the information contained therein, a second time! I realized that all this man had to do was to file a Habeas Corpus Petition with the County Court! The Court that was in this area, the one in which we were now residing! I did not want to get his hopes up, so I took it real slow and easy with him! I told him that he was going to have to give me some more information, which we were going to need in order to bring your case back into the courts! I then told him that we were going to talk it over in detail this evening after dinner! As I thought it over, I realized that all I had to do was to get his father to get a copy of the bill of sell, which proved that he actually owned the cow in question, file a Habeas Corpus Petition with the courts, then send him back into the courts, he couldn't loose the case! They would have to cut him loose, directly from the courthouse! As he had not broken any kind of law! At All! THIS WAS WHAT ATTORNEY'S CALLED A SLAM DUNK!

My man Robert couldn't wait until dinner was over, he even had his homie's to reserve my place for me in the dinner line! When a person butts someone in the dinner line they were unquestionably top notched people, who were extremely well connected! You can be damned sure that the Country Boy's Organization in this prison were extremely well connected and not to be messed with! They had at least twenty five people in this prison alone that were going to be here for the rest of the natural life and you can be damned sure that those who were going to be here for life did not give a damn about getting a murder case added onto their records! Therefore they more or less ran this prison! Also it was definitely more of them than any other group of people that were locked up in this institution, which gave them added strength! After dinner, Robert and several of his partners came and gathered around my bunk! I told Robert to give me his sister's name and address, since he said that his father could not read or write! He told me that his sister only lived a few miles away from their father, it is a know fact, that country people don't give a damn about walking several miles, just to say hello to a family member and since she was one of those who taught herself how to read and write, I neatly printer her a letter telling her to go and get the bill of sale for the cow in which her brother had been arrested, get it copied five times! Send him two of the copies of the bill of sale! Hold on to the rest, put them in a safe place just in case he needed them! It took just about two weeks before Robert came running, I knew that he had gotten the necessary documents, which we were going to need in order to get him out of here! As I looked the documents over, I realized that Gale, his sister, not only sent the two copies that we needed and told her to send to us, but she had also sent the original bill of sale! The very next day I went to the law library and got the necessary forms that I was going to need in order to send this case back into the Courts on a Habeas Corpus Petition! Taking my time, I made sure that I did not miss one single sentence that every question was completely filled out! Then I made him take his time printing his name over and over again, until we were both sure that he knew how to do so almost perfectly! Then, I told him to sign his own name to his own paperwork after I had it properly filled out, this made him beam with pride! He started saying that he was going to be going home to his home/boy's! We all were truthfully wishing him the very best of luck at the thought of this happening! This would be the first person that I had assisted in getting them their freedom back! I knew that this man did not want to be locked up in this place like some kind of an animal, especially when we all knew that he had not broken any kind of law! You can be damned sure that I, of all people, could understand how he was feeling! They had sentenced him to serve ten years and they had sentenced me to serve seven! We were kindred spirits! Since the law library was closed on Sundays, and since I was not about that dumb stuff, like lifting weights, playing basketball, horseshoes, ping-pong, jogging around the prison, or shadow boxing with the other inmates, my Sundays were filled with my going to Sunday school, followed by morning church services, followed by afternoon church services! I did not ever intend to change this method of operation, which I found myself actually liking, because as the preacher that came into our church used to always say, if you draw near unto GOD, he will draw near unto you! I personally sent up several prayers, during church services that this man, Robert Anderson, would get to go back home to his family! His mother had just passed on and his father needed him desperately! The following Monday morning, Robert, several of his home Boy's and I, went to the post office, where we sent everything that we felt would be necessary to the Circuit Court! All that we could do was to say a prayer and wait! Time slowly went by, we were all listening for the name of Robert Anderson to be called out every day that the mail was called. I went back to doing my personal researching for my own case, realizing that no matter how hard we all wanted to hear Robert's name called, the system moves extremely slow and even slower than that, when it comes to cleaning up one of their own violations! We all kept the faith, like I always told them, GOD sits high and looks low! He can and will do everything, but fail, you will see! Hold on and have faith in him! I guess that they were actually listening to me, because they started coming out to church in records numbers! We even started forming prayer groups where we would fast and pray from sundown Friday's through sundown Sunday's! We knew that there was absolutely nothing that we could do by ourselves, but together, we could possibly get the attention of our creator, All Mighty GOD! The more we continued in this manner the better it got for everyone concerned! The fighting and petty arguing in the prison, which we were being housed in, suddenly stopped! There was a kind of peace that came over us as we continued in our worshiping, the kind of peace that even we ourselves could not explain! The days all seemed to gently glide by, church services were constantly being filled to capacity with inmates, who had never came to a church service before! In my heart, I knew, that the Warden of this institution was going to have to do something quickly, because these inmates were not allowing anything negative to take control of them, as we were all putting our trust in our GOD! Day's went by, which turned into weeks, then weeks turned into months, after approximately five or six months had passed I think that just about everyone had almost forgotten about the fact that our now christen brother, Robert Anderson still yet had his court documents pending, we were all so deeply involved in our walk with our creator, and were living such a calm caring life, until we were all, more or less shocked when they called out brother Robert Anderson's name one evening at mail call! We all shouted out PRAISE THE LORD! He slowly went to get the letter, which we all saw had the courts markings on it!

Someone shouted out, IT LOOKS LIE YOU DON'T WANT THAT MAIL BROTHER ANDERSON! We all busted out laughing! As brother Anderson brought the letter back to me, my hands started shaking, as I slowly opened it! He was waiting for the expression on my face to change one way or the other, you can be sure that I did not let him down, as I shouted out PRAISE GOD!

BROTHER ANDERSON YOU ARE GOING TO BE GOING BACK INTO THE COURT WITH YOUR CASE! IN THREE DAYS! MY BROTHER! GOD IS GOING TO SET YOU FREE! HE HAS HEARD YOUR PRAYERS! I don't think that there was a single person in this jailhouse, which we were being housed in, that was not crying like a baby! I know for a fact that I was! The next three days were filled with nothing but a constant bombardment of legal questions for brother Anderson!

We all made him practice, responding to every question that we could possibly think of, which they might throw at him! We even threw questions in there that we knew they more than likely were not going to be asking him! Every inmate that was in our section of the prison came to him and questioned him! We questioned him when he was taking a shower, we questioned him when he was using the stool, we questioned him when he was attempting to go to bed at night, simply because we wanted to see how he would respond to the questioning when he was sleepy and rest broken! By the time that we had finished firing questions at him during those final day's before his case was returned to the court, we were all sure that what ever they asked him, he had definitely already heard! It was now all up to GOD and him! The morning that he was going to be departing for the Court House, he had to get up at six o'clock in the morning for his short trip, (three miles) to the courthouse! I am positive that no one but Brother Robert Anderson got any sleep that night! Before he walked out of the prison doors, the next morning, we all banned together, got down on our knees and said a prayer, asking GOD to please send this brother home to his family! Shortly after we finished our prayers, they took brother Robert Anderson away, to the waiting bus! He stopped and waved at us just before he boarded! That was the last time that any of us ever saw brother Robert Anderson in this prison ever again! Approximately three weeks later, his sister sent me and a few of the other inmates, a letter with his picture inside! She said that he was doing just fine, working his father's farm! In the picture, he was sitting on his father's front porch, eating one of his very own home grown watermelons, just like he said that he was going to do! PRAISE GOD! The very next day, The Warden of the prison sent for me to come to his office. Upon my arrival, he told me that he had heard of what I have done and what I am doing to his inmates, giving them false hopes, putting those bullshit ideas into their heads! Having them to get down on their knees and pray! He then said this is not the kind of institution that I have been sent here to run! You are going to have to stop with your Christian belief bullshit right here and right now! Because if you continue on in your present manner of talking your shit to my inmates, I am going to ship your black ass as far away from here as I can possibly get you! You can be damned sure that my guards are keeping their eyes dead on your black ass! Now get the fuck out of here! As I went through the door, exiting his office, I said a silent prayer asking GOD to touch his heart! As I headed back toward the men's detention area from the Wardens office, it suddenly dawned on me that I had now been illegally taken away from my wife and children, at this moment, for more than fourteen months and counting, I then felt anger rising in my mind as I though to myself, when is GOD going to see how hard I am trying to help others, then release me from this crazy situation that I am in? The real bitch of it all is that in my heart, I knew that I have not broken any law of any kind, according to the WRITTEN LAWS, AS WELL AS THE CONSTITUTION OF THE UNITED STATES! THIS IS NOT JUST ME STATING THESE FACTS!! DAMN!!! I knew that I had to get my mind off of the outside world and stay focused on the life which I am being forced to deal with, right here, right now, in order to survive this total nightmare! As I returned to the detention area, several of the members of The Country Boy's Organization came to me saying their leader wanted to have a talk with me! I saw nothing wrong with doing this, especially since I had been one of the driving forces behind getting one of their own people sent home! I was told to follow them, as they went over to the opposite side of the prison yard! Once we arrived to where we were supposed to have our meeting with the leader of The Country Boy's, I did not see anyone that I recognized, then I saw one of the inmates that used to always sit quietly when we were going to church, he never said anything, but was constantly watching! I often wondered who their actual leader was, I also realized that he was by no means a person to be taken lightly, so I decided to just keep my mouth shut and let whoever it was that sent for me do the talking! The inmates that brought me over here had long since gone, leaving me standing here! All of a sudden one of my closest prayer partners came walking up, he had a smile on his face as he grabbed me and pulled me close to him, hugging me as if we were about to never see each other again, and I was his little brother! His name was Larry Waldent, (A.K.A.) Scarp Iron! These men never called each other by their birth names, they always had a nickname that they went by, or their leader would give them one! In which he felt fitted them. Whatever name he decided that they were going to have, that was it! They would actually go to their death fighting to protect that name! As it was an honor to be tagged, as they called it! When Scrap Iron finished hugging me, he told me to sit down on his personal bench! This, in prison terminology, was one of the highest honors that a person could have bestowed on them by a crew leader! He did this while the whole inmate population was looking on! You can be very sure that this kind of thing spread throughout the different prisons within the State of Georgia in less than an hours time, by way of the inmate Grape Vine! When he allowed me to sit on his personal bench, this meant that from this second on, wherever I went within the walls of this prison, or any prison through out the State of Georgia, I have been blessed and accepted into the Country Boy's Nation, that no body could, or would mess with me in any manner what so ever! Now I realized that I was totally free to do my researching of the laws without having to worry about looking over my shoulder ever again! Or so I thought!

I really did not know how many inmates inside of this prison, as well as the many other prisons, throughout the State of Georgia were hooked up with the Country Boy's Nation, but I definitely had heard of them and from what I had heard, they were not the kind of people that you might want to be angry with you! Many of their members were doing natural life, in fact, the only way that you could move up in their ranks was only when you were sentenced to serve the rest of your natural life behind these walls! Therefore, I considered it an honor to be sitting down on the actual leader of their nations personal bench! When Scrap Iron sat down next to me, the whole inmate population suddenly got real quiet! As all eyes as well as ears were on us! He told me that he was real proud of how I had helped one of his family members out of this shit! He told me that Robert Anderson is his blood cousin and that what I have done would follow me for as long as I was behind these or any other prison walls in the State of Georgia! Then he told me that my new nick name from this moment on would be F. Lee Baily, because you are now an official prison lawyer and wherever you go for as long as you are serving time you will be recognized as such! Then he assigned four of his personal hand picked members to be my bodyguards! Telling them that if anything ever happens to him for as long as he is in this prison and you four are not dead, you can bet that you soon will be!

He then told me to come and go for a walk with him; there were some things that he wanted to talk over with me in private! As we walked, he told me, that if there was anything that he could do that would make my time here more comfortable, for me to just let him know, tell any one of my body guards and they would let him know! He assured me that I would never have any problems from any of the inmates locked in here at any time! Then he told me that I could get ready because he had already made arrangements for me to work in the law library on a daily basis! That my bodyguards were assigned to work there as janitors so that I would be well protected! Finally, he told me that when I went back to the detention area for lock down, I was going to be moved down to the first floor into one of the cells that had a prime view of the television! I personally could not believe what I was hearing! He then said from this point on, you are one of the chosen few who are to always enter into the eating area before the rest of the population does, you are to go directly into the chow hall and get your meal straight from the head server! Which let the whole prison know that I definitely have what is called juice! My time behind prison walls was never the same after my conversation with Scrap Iron! Everything that he said would happen did happen! I never waited in line to get my meals again, my food was always fresh and hot! Whenever I went to take a shower, the whole shower was cleared out! I took my shower by myself! Everywhere I went I always had four bodyguards with me! My clothes were always starched and pressed, neatly laid at the foot of my bed every morning! My boots were always taken away after I came in for the evening! When they arrived back at my cell they were always spit shined to an extremely high gloss! They were always returned to me before the lights were turned out for the night! A real nice stereo system was simply sent into my cell! The person who was living in the cell that I now lived in, simply was told to get his shit and move out by my newly assigned bodyguards! The other inmates that used to have prayers with me, started asking me if we were ever going to have fasting and prayers again? I sent the message by one of my bodyguards that if they still wanted to take it to GOD in prayer, I would consider it an honor to do so! When I came in from working in the law library the following evening, my old group of prayer partners were waiting on me! As we started out with our regular studying of the bible, asking each other questions and praying, I noticed that our regular group had almost doubled in size! Praise GOD! I knew that something as good as the way that we were giving GOD the praise that was due to him, was not going to last very long! The moment that I saw those two correctional officers walk into the area that we were praying and discussing GOD'S goodness, I realized in my heart that life the way that we had grown to know it, was about to change! They told me that the Warden wanted to have a little bit of a conversation with me! They were smiling as they said it! I actually felt butterflies in my stomach as I got up from the floor and went with them! When we entered the wardens office, the Warden told the correction officers that they could wait for me outside in the yard area, because what he had to say to me, he did not want anybody else to be able to repeat one single word of that which he was going to say! The correctional officers then left, he then got up from behind his desk, closed the office door, then asked me if I was out of my mother fucking mind, or was I just a damned fool? I didn't know what he meant by asking these kinds of questions, so I didn't know how to respond to it! He then told me that it was he that told the so-called leader of the Country Boy's to wrap his arms of protection around me! It is him alone that runs this damned prison! If I didn't believe him, all that I had to do was to continue with this bullshit as far as getting his inmates to go back to this so-called GOD! He then said, just so that you will know that I am the real man up in here, you are from this minute on, going to be living in another cell block where they don't give a damn about you or your beliefs! He then said, just so you will know that I am actually the man in here, I am having your shit moved as we speak! Then he said, if you go over to this cell block with that praise the lord bullshit, I am no longer going to tolerate your shit, I am then going to send your black ass to where I know for a fact that they won't allow you to talk that shit! Then, he said for me to get my black ass out of his office! NOW!

Since I had been locked behind prison walls I had only been inside of these walls and to be truthful with you I really did not want to get transferred to another prison! But, in my heart I knew that there was absolutely NO-WAY I was going to allow this racist GOD HATING white man to intimidate me to the point where I was going to stop praising my GOD! NO-WAY! When I was taken back to the detention area I was told that I needed to get my personal belongings from the correctional officers desk because I had been transferred to another cellblock, per orders of The Warden! As I was packing up the final few personal belongings that I had acquired during my stay at this prison, my so-called bodyguards were no where to be seen! I just kept quiet and continued gathering up my personal belongings! I even left the stereo unit behind, telling the guard on duty that it was not mine and whoever it belonged to would be coming for it, I am sure of that! All of my prayer partners gathered around me, laying their hands on me and simply saying a final farewell prayer! We all had tears freely flowing down our faces as I slung the few items which I had acquired over my shoulder and headed out of the door toward my new cell block! When I walked into this new cell block, looking around, I saw several of the inmates that I already knew of from just being down here, this let me know that no matter where the Warden send me, as long as I am behind these prison walls, I am going to know of some people! As I once again looked around the cell block, I even saw a few of the brothers who I prayed with on quite a few occasions during church services! The correctional officer that took me to my cell told me that I more than likely still had my job in the law library, but that I knew that everybody was now looking at me just to see what you are going to do! I then told him that if he would ever seriously study the bible, he would clearly see that men have been beheaded for worshiping GOD ALMIGHTY! So who am I to worry about being transferred to another prison for giving my GOD the glory? I am not breaking the law in any manner whatsoever! I TAKE MY PRAYERS VERY SERIOUS, JUST AS SERIOUS AS THE MUSLIM BROTHERS WHO ARE LOCKED IN HERE! THEY ARE ALLOWED TO TAKE A FIFTEEN-MINUTE PRAYER BREAK, FIVE TIMES A DAY! I AM NOT ASKING FOR MUCH! ALL THAT I WANT TO DO IS TO MAKE MY PEACE WITH MY CREATOR! GOD ALMIGHTY! IN PEACE! AND ON MY OWN TIME! I AM NOT ASKING FOR

ANYTHING SPECIAL! WHY AM I BEING SINGLED OUT! The Correctional Officer then said, Just maybe you needed to think of what it actually is that you are doing! YOU are teaching these men how to find and seek GOD! Some of them actually do find GOD, and that's real good, but there are some of them who fake like they have found GOD and will use it to their benefit and will work their way out of a place like this, then they will get out and possibly murder a whole family. Now how would you feel if that was your family? I told him, IF ALL MIGHTY GOD WANTS YOU TO COME ON HOME, THERE AIN'T NO PLACE ON EARTH THAT IS GOING TO HIDE YOU! IF IT IS GOD'S WILL, HIS WILL BE DONE ON EARTH AS IT IS IN HEAVEN! NOT YOUR WILL, NOT MINE, BUT ALL MIGHT GOD! IF HE WANTS TO CALL YOU HOME BY THE FAMILY, OR BY THE AIRPLANE LOAD SO BE IT! WHAT WE ALL NEED TO DO IS LEARN HOW TO STAY PRAYED UP! AND WALK IN GODS FAVOR! He could only shake his head as he turned and walked away!

My new cell number was now 155, and in the other building it was 100. As in every room, or cell, that they have taken me to throughout this ordeal, I have and will start my stay therein with an opening prayer and a reading of a full chapter in The Bible! This was just my way of keeping my GOD first and foremost in my heart! As I was finishing up with the reading of my Bible chapter, I heard someone that had suddenly appeared at my cell door. They got my attention by softly whispering; excuse me, Mr. F. Lee Bailey, can I come into your room? I didn't know who it was, so I told them to come on in! As he came in, I realized that he was a she! I felt that I was somewhat qualified to deal with anything, I just knew that I was not going to be able to deal with this kind of bullshit, I knew that the main thing that I had to do was to be cool and keep a level head! I just stood my ground and looked at her/him! She told me that her name was Ruby Red! She had on a pair of black stockings, tight cut off blue jeans, cool-aid, around her eyes, and a white tank top for a shirt! She even had on some female perfume and you could tell that whoever her husband or pimp was, he spent cash money on her/him! I asked her who had sent her and what did she want? She/he told me that her husband sent her over to me to see if I wanted my dick sucked! I then asked her/ him who her/his man was and she/he told me he was none other than SCRAP-IRON! I told her/him to tell your old man that I said thanks but no thanks! She/he smiled as she/he was about to leave, then she/he stopped and said too bad, because we really could have had a

32

good time! Then I told her/him GOD BLESS YOU!! I DON'T GO THAT WAY! The next morning, as I was getting ready to go to work at the library, someone knocked on my cell door! As I answered it, I saw that it was none other than Scrap Iron, he wanted to say that he thank me for not disrespecting his woman yesterday, by cursing her out or anything like that! I told him that I didn't go that way, but if I were in his shoes walking off natural life, I would more than likely have me a wife too! He smiled and said thanks for understanding! What he really wanted to know was how did I know how to get his cousin back out on the streets? I told him that I would tell him all about it this evening when I returned from the law library, doing my job! He then told me that if I didn't want to go to that place today, I didn't have to! I then told him that if I didn't go to this place, the way that I do, you can be damned sure that your cousin wouldn't have been set free! He then stepped aside and said please get the fuck out of here! As I left the detention area I got the distinct feeling that Scrap Iron was actually interested in learning the field of law. I definitely would be willing to teach him that which I had learned so far, since he was one of the lifer's in this prison! However, it would take quite a bunch of his and my time, plus a hell of a lot of dedication on his part! I knew in my heart that he would more than likely be letting me know more of what he wants to do with the rest of his life this evening! As my work assignment day was about to come to it's end, I was just a little bit curious to finding out exactly what Scrap Iron's intentions were! Once I entered the detention area, the first persons voice I heard was that of his, as he called out hey, Mr. F. Lee Bailey, Attorney of Law, come over to my cell a minute! As I arrived at his cell doorway, I was completely amazed at what I saw there in! He had a twenty-five inch color television on a night stand in one corner of his cell! He had a remote controlled, one hundred watt stereo unit on his night stand in the other corner of his cell! He had silk sheets on the regular sized bed, which was in his cell! He had a custom made towel rack built into the walls of his cell with matching towels on the racks! His room windows were tinted so that the light wouldn't bother his eyes in the daytime! He even had five quarts of whiskey on a rack over the head of his bed! With a poster of Hallie Berry on the wall directly over the foot of his bed! This inmate even had two chairs for his guest to sit in up against the wall, and just above the chairs, he had a small strobe light for when he was feeing in the mood to entertain his special company! This man was living the black mans all American dream! A flashback came to my mind of what the Warden told me, which was, that he, ran this prison,

Scrap Iron was one of his puppets! I could tell that he was at the very least, well connected to someone special, because nobody lived in this manner while doing prison time! I had all of the respect in the world for a person that could live better in prison than most people could, who were in the so-called free world! The rest of the day I found myself wondering how could this be done? For the life of me, I could not figure it out! I realized that with time everything comes to the light! So I just continued doing my assigned job while still working in the prison law library! At five thirty in the evening my daily assignment was finished and I had this day, researched and found five more violations that would be beneficial to my case, according to the laws! As the day was slowly coming to a close, I really wanted to get to my cell and start adding these violations to the Legal Brief, which I was in the process of bringing together! As soon as I turned the very last corner that brought my cell into view, one of the inmates who was definitely a member of the Country Boys Crew, came up to me and said, as soon as I finished doing whatever it was that I had to do, after my hard day at work, I should go over to Scrap Irons cell for visitation purposes! I told him that I had intentions of doing just that! He immediately disappeared from my sight, probably informing his leader, Scrap Iron, of the fact that he had done his assignment! It was at this point that I had a real sharp pain in my chest! I thought that it was gas or something like that, so I sat still for a while, then said a prayer, as the pain slowly subsided, I continued on with that which I was doing, at which point this pain completely went away! After I finished washing away the dirt from this day's activity off my body, then changing my dirty clothes, I went to see what Scrap Iron wanted! He asked me if I was interested in possibly making both of us some real money? I jokingly asked him who was it that he wanted taken out! He told me that there was a new inmate who had been railroaded into the prison system just like so many others had been, but the difference in this inmate and the others, was that he came from a very wealthy family! Who was willing to pay any amount of money to get their little baby back home! Then he said if I was to do one of those magic acts for him, like I did for his cousin, we both could be living large! I then told him that I would have to actually check into his case before I could give him, you, or anybody else, a firm commitment as to if I can help him or not! Then he asked me to tell him when and where we could meet for this conversation to take place? I told him that if this person could file a request to come to the law library tomorrow, we could discuss his case in detail! Do you think that you can hook

34

this up? He smiled and said that he will be there tomorrow at around nine thirty A.M., I then said that we will see what happens tomorrow, tell him to ask for Smitty! I then told Scrap Iron that I had to go back to my cell because I had found those five additions to add onto my case, I am continuing to prepare my Brief Of Law, to send to the United States Federal District Court! He smiled and said my brother, I truly am going to miss you when you leave us behind, but I swear, that I will always tell those that come in here behind you of the actual legend that you will be leaving behind! He then said Smitty, man, you are really inspiring a hell of a lot of these inmates to check over their cases! Also, they are starting to do a hell of a lot more reading of the laws now, and if you don't do nothing else for one more person, you have awaken their minds and for this alone, I thank you! Before I left his cell, I asked him, what ever happened to my protection that you assigned me? He said that he was now my protector and that I won't ever have to worry about being protected again, for as long as I was in this prison! As I was leaving, I saw Scrap Iron's love interest as she/he was coming up to see him! When I arrived back to my cell, I started writing the newly obtained information down in the Brief of Law, which I was formulating as I was doing this, I heard a knock on my door, I went to see who it was, when I opened the cell door, I realized that I didn't know who this person was, that was standing there, then, when I saw the brand new boots that he was wearing, I then realized that his must be the new inmate that Scrap Iron was talking about! I asked him to come on in and tell me what's on your mind? He said that he was, as I had expected, sent over to talk with me by Mr. Scrappy! I smiled at the way that he spoke, with that deep southern drawl! I told him that I didn't think I would be seeing you until tomorrow! But since you are here, come on in so that you can tell me all about how you have been fucked over by the system! Unlike my friend, Scrap Iron, I only had one chair in my cell, it was bolted to the floor! However, this was the place in which I was forced to call my home for the next seven years! I also had what was called a desk, which was just an 8 inch by 10 inch board that was attached to the walls with brackets, which would surely break if any excess pressure was ever applied to it! Finally, I had a toilet, face bowl and a twin sized bunk bed to sleep in! This was all, but this was all that I actually needed! Because from where I stood, I didn't need all of the luxuries that life had to offer me, while in prison, in my heart I was determined, to somehow make the justice system, see the errors of their ways LEGALLY! My new guest name was Marvin Maxcy, he was a short, skinny, sandy haired young white man, who I estimated to be about thirty-five years old! The word around the prison was that his family was one of those, who had a whole lot of property and money! When he entered into my cell, I immediately made my house rules crystal clear to him, which were: NEVER TOUCH ANYTHING, THAT I HAVE OUT IN HERE, SUCH AS AND NOT LIMITED TO, MY PAPERS, MY FOOD, OR ON THOSE RARE OCCASIONS THAT I AM ABLE TO GET THEM, MY SNACKS THAT I GET BROUGHT TO ME BY OTHER INMATES! IS THIS ALL THE WAY CLEAR TO YOU? He said that he understood! I then invited him to once again have a seat and start talking! As he took the seat he said, that he didn't know where to begin! Realizing that I was going to have to take control of this conversation, I asked him, to first of all, tell me exactly, what your charges are! He said, that the police stopped him, because he was in a known drug area, in the city of Atlanta Georgia! He swore to me that he did not have any drugs on him! But that he was definitely there looking to cop some CRACK! When the police put him into their squad car, they ran a background check on him, it came back, that he was one of the people, that they were looking for, who had been involved in a stick up, in which three people were killed! He swore to me that they had made a terrible mistake! I asked him, to tell me, exactly what makes you, not be the one that they were looking for? His answer actually shocked and amazed me, as he told me, that he had only recently been given an Other Than Honorable Discharge from the military, the crime that they were saying he had committed, couldn't have possibly happed by me, because, when this crime took place, more than two years ago, I was still in the Army and I was in Korea! I then said that if this is the truth, tell me, why didn't this fact get brought up in court?

He said, the attorney his family had gotten to represent him was one of his ex-girlfriends, who he broke off their relationship, just before he went into the military, after he found out that she was fucking the whole basketball team and that he had broken it off with her more than eight years ago! When he came back home, he had gotten married, to his current wife, who was Korean! I asked him, how long had he been away in the military? He said that he had planned on making it into a career, but they had caught him smoking reefer, just before he had completed his second tour of duty and kicked him out, just short of him finishing his eighth year! I then told him, that it was going to cost him, two thousand dollars, for me to help get your case back into the courts! Also, that there was no such thing as a guarantee associated with my work, but, if what you have just told me is the truth, I am positive, that I can get your case back into court, as well as get you your freedom back! But, you are going to have to trust me and do everything that I tell you to do, when I tell you to do it! Do you understand what I have just said to you! His answer was a resounding yes! Mr. Smith, I swear, that I will do whatever it takes and I will follow your every word! You will see! I then told him that under no circumstance was he to say one single word, about the fact that I, was going to help him, to anybody! If I hear anything about this, I will instantly drop your ass, like you have the plague! He then assured me, that he will and would do everything that I tell him to do, no matter what! I then printed out several instructions on a sheet of legal writing paper, which were as follows:

1.) Make your family send you copies of your discharge papers!

2.) Get them to send you approximately 10 of your most recent pictures, the ones with the date attached to the bottom of the picture, All Kodak Pictures Have This Feature!

3.) Get a copy of all of your wife's papers that show when, where and on what date you TWO were allowed to leave Korea!

4.) Get a copy of your marriage certificate, the one that you were issued when you two said your wedding vows over in Korea, along with the pictures of this blessed event!

5.) Have your wife to get the ticket stubs from the flight that you two used when you were coming back into this country, have them Xeroxed and a copy sent to you!

6.) After you have gathered all of this paperwork together, bring it all to me then we will proceed to the next step!

As my newfound friend, departed from my cell, he had a smile on his face and a song in his heart! I didn't want to tell him, that this was more than likely, going to have him confined to this prison, for at/least another one to two years, in the fighting of this case! However, it was either my help, or NO help! Fight Back or do ALL OF THE TIME! I truly did feel in my heart, that this was just another person that the system had railroaded into its ugly grip's! If it was GOD'S will, I was going to be the one, that was going to get this man, his freedom back!

The next morning, as I was getting ready to go to my job assignment, I intentionally left approximately ten minutes early, so that I could go by Scrap Iron's cell, to let him know, of how much money we were going to make from this new client! As I arrived at his door, he saw me before I arrived and opened the door, as wide as it could open! Flashing that know all smile, that he normally wore on his face! As I approached his cell door, he told me to come on in, he had been waiting on me! As I entered, he told me to tell him all about it and don't leave out one damned word! I told him, that we were going to make two thousand dollars from this deal, that his cut would be five hundred dollars! This took his breath away, he immediately got up from his chair, telling me to have a seat, in the chair of honor! I told him, that I had to go, so that I could get started, on getting the motions and other paperwork together, which I was going to be needing! He just kept smiling and said, man Smitty, you truly are the real motherfucker and your legend is growing, by leaps and bounds! I told him, that I will stop by this evening and fill him in, on all of the details, as soon as I finish up, with my work assignment! As I walked out the door, he hollered, IT AIN'T YOU THAT NEEDS BODY GUARDS, IT IS THE DAMNED SYSTEM THAT NEEDS THE PROTECTION FROM YOUR BLACK ASS! I only smiled and kept on going! I think, that we both realized, that we very well could have a booming business and WE were the only hope, of those who were railroaded, ever getting freed from this bullshit again! Also, while they were still yet confined in this prison, I could direct them to finding out; WHAT IT FEELS LIKE TO HAVE A PERSONAL RELATIONSHIP WITH GOD ALMIGHTY! Because part of my deal, for working on anybody's case, was that they were to be in church, every Sunday morning, for Sunday school, throughout the afternoon church services! NO – EXCUSES – ALLOWED! That evening, when I returned back to my cell, I kind of half way expected to see somebody standing around my cell, but, I did not expect that the actual chief of The Country Boy's Nation, himself would be standing there! As I walked up to my cell door, he told me that he couldn't wait, to hear of how we were going to be getting that kind of money, from the new inmate, who he sent to me? Then he asked me to tell him how I was going to get that kind of money brought into this prison without attracting anyone's suspicion? I then told him, that I had every intention, of having our new client, to have his family, to send my family, several postal money orders, which would total the two thousand dollars! Then, my family would send your chosen family member your cut of the money,

38

who in turn, would send you your cut of the money directly from their house! Which would make everything clean, legal and untraceable! He said man Smitty, you are the very best, that I have ever seen or heard of, in the ten years that I have been locked up in this place! Then he said exactly what I thought he was going to eventually say, which was, man, Smitty, we could actually get serious bank from turning these cases around in this place! Then he said, man with your brains and the hook up's that I have, the sky is the mother-fucking limit! You could actually come out of here smelling sweeter than a rose! With real money in your pockets! This time, it was my turn, to just smile at him and shake my head in approval! Then, it also dawned on him that he could actually send his real wife and their child, the support money that he knew they needed, as well as wanted! Tears actually started rolling down his face at this thought! At this point, I told him, that I wanted to do something even better than this, which was, why don't you let me train you, on how you send a case back into the courts yourself! This way, even if they send me to another prison, you will be able to always make yourself some real money, as well as be able to help out those, that you feel deserve to be helped! Scraped Iron could only look at me, as I saw total admiration in his eye's, the tears freely fell from them, he said that his mind told him that I was the best thing that could have ever happened to him! I then told him that once I finish training you as to how to research the various laws and how to bring them together in a legal format, you can file a motion requesting that the courts send you a copy of your case and you will be able to find out where they have violated you and your constitutional rights! Then, you can bring your own case back into the courts and if you are right, in the violations which you present, you will win your freedom back! You can be DAMNED SURE THAT YOU WERE VIOLATED IN SOME MANNER OR THE OTHER! THIS YOU CAN BET ON! SIMPLY BECAUSE YOU ARE BLACK!

I could see that he was now seriously thinking over what I had just said to him, then he looked as deep into my eyes, as humanly possible and said man Smitty, if you show me how to do this, I swear, that I will name my next child after you! He then said, that he was going to be leaving for tonight that we could and would definitely be talking some more about this tomorrow! He now had something to look forward to, I realized that he now had a real dream to cling on to, probably for the first time since his arrival in this place, more than ten years ago! As I said my prayers that night, you can be sure that I lifted up several special requests to my (GOD-ALMIGHTY) Asking him to please, continue blessing me, so that I, can continue being a blessing to those that are railroaded into this place! As strange as this may sound, I somehow got a special feeling that particular night, just as I was almost finished with that particular prayer, which somehow made me feel, as if what I was doing, was in GOD'S WILL! When I woke up the next morning, right after I finished taking my shower, as I was putting on the prison outfit that I had intentions of wearing that particular day, I heard a gentle knocking on my cell door, I immediately responded with the fact, that whoever it was, they were going to have to wait, until I finish putting on my paints, before I will be able to answer the door, that is, unless you are the Warden, or a Correctional Officer! Since the door was not opened, by a member of the staff, using their keys, I assumed that it was just another inmate, like myself! When I was able to answer the door, I was actually shocked to see none other than my now new partner in the legal business, Scrap Iron, he was all dressed and ready to go to his first beginners class, so that he could learn the fine arts of researching the various laws, by way of Shepherdizing The Case Laws, Marshaling The Facts Together, as well as how to be able to present that which he had gathered, for the various courts, putting it into a Legal Format, before sending it to any court of law! I personally had every intention of teaching those that I worked with, everything that I possibly had learned, as well as that, which were at our disposal! Then showing them exactly how to study, garnering only the necessary and vital material from all study lessons, after which, I was going to have them to study on their own, to demonstrate that they understood that which I was teaching! Finally, I had intentions of regularly testing them, to find out just how much of our studies they were retaining! As long as the powers that be held me under this illegal confinement! I had made it up in my mind that I was going to now show every inmate that was teachable, how to fight the system back, I was going to do this quietly, not drawing any kind of attention to myself of any kind! My intention was to actually teach those who were teachable, of exactly how the courts railroaded people into its prisons! Then teach them of how to file a HABEAS CORPUS PETITION, In Any and all Courts, from City Courts, all the way up to THE SUPREME COURT OF THE UNITED STATES OF AMERICA! However, my immediate goal was to simply teach these first two inmates of how to fight the system back! Making those two promise, to teach two more, making those two promise, to teach two more and so on! That way, the Correctional Officers would not actually notice that the inmates are getting smarter, until it was too late to do anything negative to any of them, I knew that once my students had obtained the knowledge of the various laws, as well as the court systems, which I intended to slowly impart upon them! It would be to late if they only learned how to do a minimal of the legal works that I intended them to know of! I realized, that if the Correctional Officers, were to find out, what I was attempting to do, they would send information of this kind, in on their daily reports, or personally go to the Warden and tell him what we were doing! Once the Warden read of what we were doing, or was told of what we were doing, he would more than likely, do something extremely drastic, like, close the Law Library down, or transfer us to separate prisons throughout The State Of Georgia! Therefore we had to act as if nothing out of the ordinary was taking place! Since my new partner, Scrap Iron, clearly showed a serious interest in learning that which I wanted to teach, I decided to allow him the opportunity, to decide who was worthy, as well as who he felt actually wanted to fight their convictions, also, he had to make sure that whoever he chose was actually smart enough to study the various laws and do so, under my guidance! From my standpoint, life in this prison, was about to become interesting, to say the very least! I realized, that slow and easy was definitely the way to go, when it came to executing this plan! Like I said earlier, I was determined to show the justice system the errors of their ways, LEGALLY! Please let me be the first one to say, that it was extremely hard teaching Scrap Iron and his partner Leon Bowers the ends and outs of the legal system, I had to constantly go over and over the subject material with them! Which I formulated to be very basic study material, both of them failed every test that I gave them, many times over, you can be damned sure that I wanted to simply stop! Letting them know that this was simply too hard for them, then, I would remember that this was their only chance at freedom! I would then push them, reminding them that if they gave up and quit they were only hurting their chances for ever getting out of this place! This would make them settle down for a little while, until I decided to give them another test, I also discovered, that if a person has never been forced to study, by willingly attending a college or some other form of higher educational institution that person does not realize or understand that he can actually achieve the good grades and is totally out of touch with the fact that they too, are very capable, therefore, they start off with that I can't do it attitude, which, for any instructor is the very hardest thing to break through!

At/least, this was the most major obstruction that I had to overcome! You can be damned sure, that on many occasions I wanted to just say fuck this shit, I have made a mistake, in thinking that I could do this! Then somehow, one of these two men, would do something like study extremely hard and get a passing grade, on their test, then say that it is only because of you Mr. Smith, that I have been able to do this! Which would make me have the desire to continue on, plus, I would remember that this actually was, their one and only chance, of ever getting out of this place! I would then struggle on! However, you can be damned sure that I will never get the urge, to take on this kind of an added responsibility again EVER! While I was attempting to teach these two men all which I had learned, pertaining to the various laws, I was also, continuing to do the work, for my newest client, which I had given my word, that I would help, plus, his family was definitely willing to send the money that we discussed, to anyone that I chose, at any given time! Which definitely, made me gravitate toward him and his problems, in a more favorable manner! As two thousand dollars was quite a lot of money when one is behind prison walls! So I continued giving my two special students various assignments, having them to research different cases, while I researched the different laws pertaining to this man's case! Approximately three months after I told my new client Marvin Maxcy of that which I expected him to get together and bring to me, he did just that! After which he asked me, was there anything else that I wanted him to do, or get?

I told him to wait, I will be looking over the material that you have brought to me before I can possibly answer that question! I will be getting back to you in approximately three days! I then told him that I am proud of how you have done so well in following my instructions, keep up the good work! I saw the smile that he was wearing not only on his face but also in his heart, as he slowly walked away! That evening, I went over the various materials that Marvin had given to me! As I looked over his information, I actually wondered, how in the hell, was this man, possibly in prison? According to these papers, which were issued by The United States Federal Government, the Military! Also, according to what these pictures clearly shows, this man was in the United States Army and was stationed in the Country Of Korea, before, during as well as after this crime was committed! What he had told me is the absolute truth, he can prove it with legally issued proof! Therefore this man was definitely innocent of the railroaded charges, which he was now confined herein for! Therefore he was telling me the truth all the time! I now realized that we were at the point where the money was going to have to change hands! Also he was going to have to sign and send The Circuit Court, this motion which I had ready and waiting on his signature, which petitioned the sentencing court to send him a copy of the transcript of his case! AS OF HIS CONSTITUTIONAL RIGHT! AT THE PUBLIC'S EXPENSE! AS HE IS AN INDIGENT STATE INMATE! As I was doing this for my client, I continued working with my now two prize students, as they both now realized that they could learn that which I was attempting to teach them and was both now getting A's and B's on their tests, which I personally gave to them! They now looked forward to my giving them, my instructions and then simply leaving them to their selves, so that they could do the assignments! Plus, I showed them how to add their own special wording and explanations, onto their legal citings of various case laws! I actually saw the pride that these two had in achieving that which they set out to accomplish! I constantly encouraged them to keep up the good work! The more they wanted to learn, the more I would show them how to seek and find, I now take personal pride, in saying that these two men, did their assignments so good until they both were able to send two convicted and sentenced inmates back into the courts, making the courts review the cases and both cases were overturned! I took personal pride, in watching them as they were growing, in their knowledge of that which I had been forced to turn to, which was the written laws that govern this great country! I knew in my heart that they were this very moment, more than qualified, to hold their own in any court of law! As they now understood what a person ment when they said a subject is moot! I personally took them to the Blacks Law Dictionary, then made them totally understand, read of, and be able to identify with every legal subject therein! This was achieved, in a brief amount of time! Both of them actually knew of how to properly present a case, in a court of law, with case laws being cited therein! This goes for the City, State and the Federal courts! They knew what it was to FILE LEGAL BRIEFS, IN A TIMELY MANNER! They know exactly how to Legally Argue a case in front of a Magistrate, a Judge, or a Judge and Jury! You can be damned sure that they had enough wisdom from their newly acquired legal skills, that they both could and would seriously confuse the hell out of a jury of their peers! Making it virtually impossible for anyone to get a clear conviction against them! Also, you can be damned sure, that I personally trained them, of how to bring a case back into any court of law! For Retrial, To

Be reheard, through the filing of Legal Motions, Subpoena's, as well as various forms of Writ's! Then, just to make sure that my first set of understudies were all the way prepared to actually litigate a case until it's total conclusion, we had mock trials, which only we attended! Then, to make sure that each one of them was totally clear of how the laws worked, I silently looked over their shoulders as they actually worked on getting more and more cases sent back into the courts! However, they had to have at least five of their clients to get their cases returned to the courts, then they had to get set free! For them to graduate from my class! They both passed my challenges with flying colors, it did wonders for my pride when I personally saw the two of them seriously smiling with open pride, as their 5th clients were both set free! We even had what we called a graduation party in Scrap Irons cell! He gladly opened up one of those bottles of whiskey that he had on the shelf over his bed! The three of us had a good time, we laughed and discussed how well qualified and knowledgable they had now become! They could now definitely be looked on as jailhouse lawyers! I also made sure that the two of them made me just one single promise, which was, they both were now going to make damned sure that they pass on that which they had learned, even if they were working on getting their own cases back into the courts! One more thing we all three were in full agreement of, was that if there was any way possible, we were all going to file Civil Actions against the State of Georgia! For the way that they have treated us and the way that we knew they treated so very many other people, especially black men! I had a real surprise for each of my star pupils whom I was so very proud of! While they were busy studying as hard as they were, I secretly sent and asked one of my brothers to send me two zeroxed copies of my College Degree, then when I received the copies I went to the Law Library and made new copies, whiting out my name, then adding their names, which meant that they both had Official Degrees with their names already affixed! They both could not believe their eyes, they were so proud until both allowed tears to freely roll down their faces! As they both truly felt as if they had actually graduated and had received their degrees! We hung out together and had what we called our party for the rest of the day! But as the night slowly rolled in, we three had to realize, that all good things must and will come to an end! As this was the case in this occasion! I let both of them know of how very proud of them that they actually made me feel and I now know for a fact, that the two of them would and could, now go forth and actually kick ass all the way to freedom!

But I once again reminded them both, remember that you now owe me, as well as yourselves, the keeping of that promise that you both made, in which you will now teach two people as you have been taught! Then, we went our separate ways, but always having a great respect for each other, with the knowledge that we all knew and realized exactly what the other person had obtained! It was heading toward the time of year that any and all inmates in any prison system hates, which were the Christmas Holidays, my client, Marvin Maxey was just like everybody else, wanting to be free from this place! Especially around the Christmas Holidays! He started to ask me if I actually knew of approximately when he was going to be going back into the courts with his case! I didn't want to be one of those who told their clients lies, so I pulled him into my cell, then told him that he had better get used to the fact that he was more than likely going to be spending this Christmas behind bars! Since the courts closed down for the holidays right around the 15th of December and did not re-open until the first week in the month of January! I too wanted to spend the holidays out in the free world, but it looks like we are all going to sing Jingle Bells back behind these walls together. I then told him that I however did have some good new for him, which was that I had finished bringing all of the legal issues together pertaining to his case and as soon as the courts reopened, after the X-Mas holidays, I was going to send in all of his information, he should be getting some kind of a response from the courts by the end of February, in the up coming year! He looked at me with sadness in his blue eyes, then asked, if I could please, put a rush of some kind on it! I told him that if he felt that he was able to put a rush on the courts, of any kind what so ever, for him to please feel free to attempt do so for yourself! Then you will see for yourself that there is no way know to man kind that you, me or anyone that we know of, can put a rush on the courts! Especially when we are already tried and convicted inmates! I kind of think that this slowly got through to him, because he started to calm down! As in every prison throughout this country, the X-mas holidays truly are the absolute worst! All that they play on the radio stations are those Damned holiday songs, which really start making a person think about their loved ones out in the Free World! Especially when the prison that you are locked in goes into a lock down mode! Which means for the whole week before and after X-mas day, the inmates are totally locked into their cells almost 24 hours a day, while that homesick ass music is piped into the prison! The Correctional Officers are in the X-Mas mood, so they turn up the music loud! However, on

X-mas day we are all treated in a real special manner, the State of Georgia awards every inmate the opportunity to spend seven dollars at their State ran stores, in appreciation for the work that you had done on behalf of the State of Georgia, throughout the previous year! The only catch was, you had to spend every penny! The Second that you were taken into their very limited store! As the Christmas holidays slowly came to their conclusions, I personally think that every inmate in any State run institution would agree with me in the fact that we are extremely happy to see them go! I didn't tell my client Marvin anything about it, but I too was waiting for the holidays to come to their conclusions, so that I too could file my own Habeas Corpus Petition in the United States Federal District Courts, hoping and praying, that they would accept, as well as grant my petition, which would release me from this madness! During the holidays, I made my once a year phones calls to my family members at an appointed time and on the appointed date! This particular day, I told one of my family members of how I was going to be having some friends of mine to send him postal money orders, I was going to have my people down here in Georgia put his name on them, he was supposed to cash the money orders, then to keep Five Hundred Dollars for himself, then send Five Hundred Dollars to the address which I gave to him, then send the remaining thousand dollars here to me in two hundred dollar money orders, one per week for the next ten weeks! The five hundred dollars that you will get for your pocket should more than cover your troubles! He immediately agreed to this offer without any kind of delay what so ever! I then told him that he was going to have to allow me to be able to call him, at any time, because I could very well be calling him to tell him of more money that I was going to be sending to him and I had to tell him how to distribute the money! He then said that if this was the way that I was going to be contacting him and if the reason was that more money was coming his way, he would be more than willing to allow my calls to come through to him, at any given time! Also, he would be willing to forward any amount of money that I tell him to forward to whoever I tell him to send it to! This was exactly what I wanted to hear from him! I wished him and his a happy new year! Which actually did not mean one single thing to me, except that the courts would be opening up again for the start of the New Year! Thank GOD! I had the word sent out from my cell that I wanted to see my client, Mr. Marvin Maxcy! Within a matter of approximately five minutes this man was standing at my cell door asking me if it was all right for him to come in! Once I approved his entry into my cell, he entered and asked me if there was anything wrong with his case? After I informed him there was nothing wrong with the case and that everything was proceeding as expected, he looked at me with wonder in his eyes, not wanting to leave my client in limbo, I explained to him that the time was right for the money to be changing hands! He looked at me and said Mr. Smitty is that all that you are calling me in here for, I told him yes, then I gave him my hand written instructions of who where and when to have the money sent! Next I sat him down and told him of what my instructions were, just so that he would definitely know what I was expecting of him and his family! As he departed from my cell door he told me that he would go and tell his people about these arrangements right away! I stood at my cell door and watched as he did just as he said that he was going to do, which was to go get on the phone and call somebody, I assumed that it was one of his family members, because when I called my family the following week, they told me that they had indeed received three postal money orders, totaling two thousand dollars exactly! I then went by my partner Scrap Iron's cell, to tell him that his money had already been sent to the address that he had given to me! He was all smiles when he heard this news! Then he said, this money would probably be enough, for him to fight this case, all the way up to The Supreme Court, Of The United States Of America! If it was necessary! I then told him that he might as well calm down and continue studying your notes, also regularly read over those tests that we took, so that you will stay dead on top of your skills, he only looked at me and said man you are damned right! That's exactly what I intend to be doing for the rest of my stay inside this place! He then said Smitty, I truly do thank you man, for seriously helping me, in more ways than you can possibly imagine, then he told me that he wanted to show me how much he actually appreciated what I have done for him! He then asked me to come on and go with him to one of HIS SPECIAL MEETINGS THAT HE, THE CHIEF OF THE COUNTRY BOY'S NATION HAS CALLED!

It goes without saying that I went with him to this meeting! His members really were smooth and quiet, while this meeting was going on! When he spoke, you could hear a pin drop! For the first time, I actually saw his leadership skills, as he told fifteen of his crew sub-leaders of what good things that we had been doing! Then he introduced me as brother James Smith (A.K.A. Smitty) saying that I was the one who kicked his cousins case back into the courts, and got him free! Then he told them that they wouldn't believe what I had done for him! He then said, I want the word to go around throughout every prison that is inside of this State, that under no circumstances will any of our people EVER violate this man in any manner what so ever! He has really shown to me, that there truly are a few good people still yet left on this earth! Then he said, my brothers, I present one of them to you right this very minute! Then He Told His Crew Leaders That I Was To Be Treated As His Brother! With Full Respect Accorded! He Told them to go and spread the word! Just Like That, his word went throughout every prison within the State Of Georgia! On The Prison Grape Vine! As we walked back toward our respective cells, all we did was to look at each other and laugh, because, we both knew, that each of us were true get down black brothers! Who were not afraid to go out and make it happen! The days slowly started to once again drift on by, then one evening at mail call, they called out the name of Marvin Maxcy, everyone knew, that it was some kind of letter from the courts, because everyone definitely recognized the courts identifying headings on the envelope! He came right over to my area before he opened up the letter, making sure that I would be able to hear his response, which would be his court date, for his scheduled Court Hearing! Just as I knew, his letter stated that he had two weeks before he was supposed to be taken back into court! He slowly eased over to me, then shyly looked at me and said, Mr. Smitty, I truly didn't believe that you really knew what you were talking about, or what you was doing, but, he wanted to apologize for the way that he was thinking! I told him to just forget about what you were thinking, because now we have to properly school you on various points of the law, so that you will be fully prepared when they start questioning you! I then told him to make damned sure that you come by my cell everyday, at five thirty in the evening, for question and answer sessions! Marvin simply shook his head in agreement!

For the next two weeks Marvin was questioned by probably ever inmate throughout the prison population! As it had become somewhat a custom for the whole population to help out any inmate, by questioning him whenever they found out that they were going back into the courts in order to have their case reheard if I was there or not! You can be sure that everybody was questioning him! As I was getting ready to go to my work assignment I saw them questioning him, when I cam back in from the finish of my day's assigned job, I saw them continuing to question him! I already knew, that his man was able to not only get the courts attention strong enough for them to bring his case back into the courts, he was more than likely already a free man, at this moment! It was just a matter of going through the formalities, which the courts truthfully did not like to do! As my client's court date slowly approached, he was constantly hanging around me for guidance, as well as moral support, of which I gave to him freely! On the actual date of his trial, he was openly crying, letting the whole inmate population know, of how it was because of what I had done for him that he was able to get his freedom back! He said that he was truly blessed, to have been brought into this prison, where I am being held! Just as they always have done, to every other inmate, on the morning that his case was to be brought back into the court! They came for him early in the morning! When they opened up his cell, he came running down to my cell, where he gave me, everything that he had obtained, while he was an inmate in this institution, such as five stamped envelopes, three writing tablets, five packages of strawberry cookies, a portable radio, with good batteries already inside, and the battery charger! He then gave me his address, zip code, and telephone number, then said that he wanted me to please call him when ever I got out of this place, he would then be able to look out for me, the way that I have so gracefully looked out for him! I then thanked him for all the good things that he was leaving for me, then told him, to be damned sure, to keep your shit together, when you go out there! We then hugged each other and had a final cry! As they called out his name! I think that we both knew, in each others heart, that this would be the very last time, that we would more than likely, every lay eyes on each other again! He looked back at me one more time, as he departed! I said a silent prayer for my friend and client, Marvin Maxcy!

Later on that same day, I saw my partner Scrap Iron, as he was coming from the Law Library, he motioned for me to come over to his cell, I could see that he had not only law books in his hands, but he had at least six brand new legal tablets, it was very apparent that he intended on doing an awful lot of legal writing! As I entered his cell, I could see that he was in the process of writing to the courts! He asked me, to help him out on a few questions that he was having, I teasingly told him, that if this attorney helps you out, with any of your questions, you are going to have to pay me, for my services, as well as my time, He said, that he would definitely be willing to do so! Mr. F. Lee Baily! We laughed, then hugged each other, as I took my seat, so that I would get comfortable, while answering the questions, that we both knew, he was going to be asking me! He actually only wanted to know, exactly who it was, that he was to send his motions to, in order to get a transcript of the case, that he was involved in! I started to talk shit and tell him, to go and look it up in the Law Library for yourself! You are a qualified jailhouse attorney, with full honors attached! I very well could have said it this way, but for some strange reason, I decided against doing this! I told him, that his motions must always be forwarded to the sentencing court, in care of the clerk of said court He looked at me with tears in his eyes, saying that he has been down here for so long, until he honestly didn't know who the clerk of the court was, or, their address! I then told him, if you go into the Law Library and ask the clerk therein, they will quickly direct you to the books, which will give you all of the information, that you could possibly need, I then told him, that we used to always discuss the fact that you might sometime need to talk over various laws and different situations, that you may not know of, saw on television, or you may not have heard of, they will be in the Law Library, or, you can find a case that is close to being like that one! You know How to research the laws, this I know for a fact, the next time that I see your ass attempting to go around the researching of the laws, by picking my brain, I am only going to tell you to go and talk it over with the clerk in the Law Library! Scrap Iron allowed me to totally finish, with my ranting and raving, then he simply said, EXCUSE ME, BUT AREN'T YOU THE CLERK IN THE LAW LIBRARY? We both busted out laughing! That evening after all of the work details were back into the detention area, they gave us an early mail call, which usually only happened if everybody fully cooperated, and there was not any kind of disruption during the count of the inmates, we were all happy to get this early mail call none the less! As usual I truly didn't expect anything from mail call, but I would always listen, to hear who was getting mail! When they called out my name, I was totally shocked and when the Correctional Officer held it up for me to come and get it, I am positive that every person in this prison realized that this was one of those packages that came from the courts, just as I also realized this fact! The whole prison got strangely quiet as I quickly came forward to claim my mail! The Correctional Officer who was handing out the mail was the one who actually broke the quietness when he said Ooh shit, Mr. F. Lee Baily is about to be leaving us all! The strangest thing was that nobody found his comment to be very funny, because not one single inmate laughed, they simply kept quiet! I on the other hand was exceptionally glad, my hands were shaking so hard, until I was not able to open up the envelope that I had

50

received, I went directly toward my cell, so that I could be by myself, when I opened and read this letter! But you can believe that this was not to be! When I went into my cell, there were at least 10 other inmates with me, without any of them ever saying one single word, just wanting to hear what my letter said! When I opened it up and read the contents, I couldn't help, but to smile at its contents! It was from The United States Federal District Courts, The Senior Judge, Of The Courts For The Ninth District! Wrote This Document! Which stated, that he personally was looking into the legal issues, which I have presented, and will be getting back into contact with me pertaining to the decision, which will be rendered, in response to these challenges, in the near future! I informed all that were in attendance of what this letter said, and that I was not getting ready to leave them at this particular time, but, it would only be a short amount of time, before I would one day, come in here, grabbing all of for my personal belongings then saying goodbye! I then started to feel, that I was getting somewhat sleepy, and though that I would just lay down and sleep, the rest of the day away! As it truly had been one of those extremely long days! Just as I had finished taking my shower and was about to close my cell door and turn off the lights, before saying my nightly prayers! Someone was at my door gently knocking, as I went and answered, it was none other than my now best friend Scrap Iron, who told me, that he heard of the bad new that I had received! That he truly felt sorry for me, and did I want a good slug from one of his ladies? (drink of whiskey) I told him that when I show you, what The Senior Judge Said, I Don't Think You Are Going To Feel Sorry For Me! As he came into my cell I quickly grabbed the letter and handed it to him! When he finished reading it he still looked puzzled, he didn't understand that a Senior Judge would or legally could send a confined inmate a written letter, pertaining to their on-going case! Truthfully in a perfect world his actions were not normal, but when any kind of a decision that was possibly going to finally go in my favor, you can be Damned Sure! That I, for one, was not going to challenge these strange actions of the court! I am once again, positive that my partner Scrap Iron was totally confused, so I told him that I would explain it all to him tomorrow! He slowly left my cell, with a not understanding look in his eyes! I personally found it hard to fall asleep that night! My mind kept on wondering, what had that document actually meant? I swear that I looked that letter over at least twenty-five times, or more, and every time that I read it over, I assumed something different! So, I decided to just let it go, then, see for myself, what the senior judge meant, in this letter, through his actions! The month of February came and left, without any changes being made on my behalf, by the courts! One day, I sat down and started adding up the time that I had been away from my family, it had been almost three years and this coming up June, it would actually be three years! Realizing that there was nothing that I personally could do, about my current situation, but pray! I continued with my prayers! I also, continued with my fasting, even though I did not, and was told not too, ever, invite any of these inmates, into my prayer sessions! That way everything would be considered all right, in the eyes of the Warden, and the Correctional Officers! Several days later, my friend Scrap Iron, once again eased back into my world! He said that, the reason he was not coming around that much any more, was because, he thought that I wanted a little bit of space, so that I could prepare the next move that I was going to make, on their asses! I then told him, that I didn't have to make anymore moves that letter from the Senior Judge made everything perfectly clear that all I had to do was be cool and wait for their decision to come down! I told him that The Senior Judge, was letting me know, that these kind of violations were against the laws, that he was personally looking into this case and in a little while, he was going to probably send a letter, or, a team of people down here and more than likely, make them let me go! My partner, Scrap Iron smiled at me, as he slowly eased himself away from me! I also smiled, as I realized, that he probably thought that I was losing it, or, I had simply started living in a fantasy world! A world in which, we both saw so many of these people in here, move into! There was a saying which we always used to say to each other, when we saw one of our friends, acting just a little bit, on the strange side, which would always get some kind of a reaction out of them, which was: They Can Fuck With Me! But They Cannot Fuck With Time!

I noticed, that I was starting to hear this quote, more and more from these inmates! It was very apparent, that they were thinking, that I was actually losing it! So I just kept quiet and stayed to myself, because, I refused to continually explain over and over again, what this letter meant, as well as repeating to these inmates, what my opinion of this letter was! Time continued rolling on by, I continued with my now job in the Law Library, also continued helping those inmates who were less fortunate than myself! I was starting to hear the rumors that were starting to circulate throughout the prison, about me, which was: He Knew How To Get Everybody Else Our From Behind These Walls But He Couldn't Do A Damn Thing

For His Own Black Ass! I even noticed, that my so-called friend Scrap Iron wouldn't even come nowhere near me anymore! In fact, as I thought about it, there wasn't nobody ever coming near me recently! Even those that used to piss me off with their nagging ass questions were avoiding me, as if something was wrong with me! I went to talk this problem over, with the Chief Of The Country Boy's Nation, None Other Than My Partner Scrap Iron! When I arrived at his cell door, he told me to come on in and have a seat! He already knew that I was going through, what was commonly known, as the silent treatment! I didn't know, who had told these inmates, to put this on me? I hadn't violated anybody that I knew of, but I knew, that if anybody knew what was going down, it surely would be Scrap Iron, my supposed to be friend and partner! I didn't have to say one single word, all that I had to do, was to simply come into his cell! He knew, exactly what was going down! He said, that he had to stop several of these people, from putting a contract on my head! I really was fucked up, at this statement and asked him to explain to me what and why, would someone want to put a hit out on me? I haven't done nothing, but try to help these people out, since my arrival! Scrap Iron then said Smitty, that's the problem! When you arrived in here, you were sending these inmates back into the courts, like you owned the courts! Now, you don't even discuss their cases with them anymore! They think that you have sold out to the system!

He said that he had made several of these inmates, back down from putting a hit out on my ass, but Smitty I don't have the eyes of GOD! Man, I am so glad, that you have now came back to see me! Even, I was starting to wonder about you! Man, you have really been going into your own world! While these people are in desperate need of you and your knowledge! Surely you can see this can't you? I had to admit, that life had been playing ugly tricks on me, and my desires for freedom! I then vowed right there and right then that I would reopen my attorneys office, also that I would be accepting new clients as soon as tomorrow morning! Scrap Iron simply smiled and asked if he could send me another client over to my cell tomorrow? I told him to send him on! When I left Scrap Iron's cell as I was walking past the showers I heard somebody who called out my name, when I turned to see who it was, everything suddenly went black, when I realized what had happened I was in the shower with four inmates surrounding me, they told me that I was a sellout to the system, as they took turns knocking the living shit out of me, I was never allowed to give any kind of an answer in my own defense, as they knocked me from one inmate to the other! When I once again regained my sight, I was laying in the hospital with tubes coming from both my arms! When the nurse saw that I was awake, she immediately ran and called the doctor, who came in to my room and gave me an immediate checking over, from head to toe, then he explained what had happened to me, he said that I had been seriously beaten by at least three to five inmates, it was touch and go with you, and for the past three days we did not know if you were going to come back to us! He told me that I would have to stay in this hospital for at least another two or three weeks! I really felt as if I had been ran over by a Mack Truck, everywhere I turned I was in severe pain! I swore at that very second that it was now me against the world! I wouldn't help another mother fucking one of these inmates to do shit, ever again! I was slowly able to tell the doctor that I was hurting all over and would he please give me something for this GOD awful pain! He smiled and said that he would be back shortly with something! Try as I may for the life of me, I couldn't remember the ass whipping, that they gave to me, or who it was, that did this to me! Everything was a complete fog, one in which I knew in my heart, I was not about to let those that were responsible, get away with this! As it was not in my nature to do so and I knew this! Time heals all wounds was now the words that were floating around inside my head! I also knew, that if I just keep quiet and keep my mouth closed, sooner or later, those that were responsible for this, were going to let it slip, from their bragging lips! Then, it would be my turn! Just like the doctor said, it took exactly three weeks, before I was able to come back to my old cell, which was not occupied by a new inmate! It felt like coming back home when I walked through that door! As I settled down and was getting ready to take my medicine and just call it a night! My old friend Scrap Iron was standing at my door asking to come in! I opened my door and told him that I didn't want to talk about it today and that once I heal up for a few days I would let him know what my intentions are! He only looked at me then said Smitty you can be damned sure that whatever you decide my crew is 100% behind you! Just go ahead and get you some rest! The day's continued to gently slip on away and I continued to recover from my injuries, I could feel my body as it was getting stronger and stronger, in my heart, I actually felt as if I was already 100% stronger at that very second, but when I attempted to lift anything, with some kind of weight to it, I then realized, that what I was doing was only wishful thinking! One evening, just as I was about to take the sleeping pills that the hospital had prescribed for me, I heard a gentle knocking at my cell door, when I opened it, one of the brothers who I used to pray with was standing at my door! I asked him what it was that he wanted? He told me that he wanted to please have a conversation with me! I allowed him to come in just so that I could hear what it was that was on his mind! As he entered into my cell he started crying and said that he was so sorry, for what had happened to me, that I didn't deserve this kind of treatment! He then told me of every single person who had been involved in jumping me! I now was definitely going to be able to get my revenge! For some strange reason, the information that this inmate had given to me, made me feel like, I was able to kick a Grizzly Bear in the ass! There was no way, that I was going to let these mother fuckers, get away with what they had done! Plus, the fact that four of them had to jump me clearly showed me, that they were nothing but punks! We had a saying down here, which I am sure, they were more than likely hearing at this very moment, which stated: IT AIN'T NO FUN WHEN THE RABBIT HAS GOT THE GUN! Which was clearly the case in this instance! Since I knew that I was going to be going to the hole after I fucked these inmates up I prepared for this event, by stocking up on my goodies like my cookies and candy bars, I even bought an extra four bars of soap, the extra large kind! I would always see, those who I knew, were responsible, for the down home ass whipping, that was given to me! They had started hanging together in groups of twos, they felt that this was going to help them if and when I came for their asses! One Friday evening just as two of them were finishing with their showers, wiping the soap from their eyes, I stepped into the shower with two bars of soap stuffed together in a pair of socks! This was my weapon of choice, which I used on their heads, as I hit the first inmate upside his head, I saw blood quickly flood from his nose, he instantly fell to the floor, in a heap, without moving anymore! The second inmate, saw what had happened, to his partner and attempted to get out of the showers by running but he didn't have shoes on his feet, which caused him to slip and fall, as he slid into one of the corners of the showers, it was now my turn and as I was beating the living shit out of him I quoted that saying: IT AIN'T NO FUN WHEN THE RABBIT HAS GOT THE GUN IS IT MOTHER FUCKER! The correctional officer on duty was making his count of us inmates for his shift to begin, and as he came by the showers he heard the noise of my getting my revenge and stopped me from actually killing those two people! I found out later on, from the segregation cell that I was thrown into, by one of the inmates whose job it was to daily clean up the segregation cells, that they both had concussions of their skulls, broken noses, several teeth were knocked out and the second one had three fractured ribs! The other two, who I had not been able to get yet, went to the Warden and confessed, telling him, that they were the other two, who had been involved in that assault on me, and they wanted to get transferred out of this prison, for their health and safety sakes, as they feared for their life! After hearing this, the Warden could not do nothing but transfer them, their confessions tied his hands, also, he had to release me from the segregation cell that he was holding me in! Early the very next morning, just as I was getting ready to go to my assigned job, one of the Correctional Officers, came to my cell and told me that, I was being summoned to come down to the Wardens Office! I just knew that he wanted me, because of the ass whipping, that I had to administer to those that violated me! However, when I arrived at his office door, I saw two strange looking men waiting inside his office, I realized that I had gotten my revenge, in a small manner of speaking, but I didn't actually kill any of those two, or had one of them died today or last night and I had not heard of it yet! My heart was beating real fast, as I entered the Wardens office! When I was inside, the older looking of these two double checked with the Warden to make sure that I was the James Soloman Smith Jr. that he was looking for, he then checked my identification card, as he was handing me back my identification card, he told The Warden that he had to leave the three of us alone and that he could not question me at any time, concerning what we discussed in this office, not ever! The Warden shook his head in agreement and quietly left his office! Once we were all alone the older of the two told me to have a seat, as I was doing this he pulled out his badge, showing me that he and his partner were both from the F.B.I. and that they were here because of what I had presented in my Brief Of Law, the one that I had presented to the United States Federal District Courts For The Ninth Circuit of the Northern District Of Georgia! Then he said Mr. Smith I assure you that the information that you have provided was read over by people in very high places and we can assure you that in a very brief amount of time you are going to be brought into the Senior Judge Of the United States Federal District Court's Office, where you will be set totally free from any and all further imprisonment! We have been sent into this prison to tell you of this before it happens so that you won't be worried when you are told to get your stuff together! He then asked me if I had any questions that I wanted answered? I responded with but only one single question which was; PLEASE TELL ME EXACTLY WHEN THIS WAS GOING TO HAPPEN? The agent from the F.B.I. told me that today is Monday! You can be sure that you will be gone from this place, by no later than Friday morning! NEVER TO RETURN! It was very hard to do, but I somehow managed to control my composure I refused to let them or anybody realized that this prison stuff was driving me absolutely crazy especially when I knew that the charges which they were holding me for was totally against The Laws as well as The Constitution Of The United States! When the agents from the F.B.I. had departed and the Warden had returned to his office, I asked him if there was anything that he wanted to discuss with me? He only looked at me then said that he would be extremely glad when my time in his prison was up! Because I truly was a pain in his ass! Then he told me to get the fuck out of his office! Once I was out of his office and was headed back toward the detention area, I couldn't help, but to allow the tears to freely roll down my face! I had to actually stop and catch my breath a few times, as what he had said, started to actually sink in! By the end of this week I was going to become a free man! PRAISE GOD!! It goes without saying that I was no longer interested in the day-to-day functions of what was taking place inside this prison! Everybody wanted to congratulate me on the way that I handled my business, when it came to dealing those who were responsible for fucking over me in the way that they had! I gratefully thanked every one of the inmates who came up to me, but I am sure that they could see that my heart was not anywhere near this place! It was at this very moment that I actually felt that I was now liked and respected for handling my business! Ain't that a BITCH! Early the next morning, one of the Correctional Officers, came to my cell and told me that I was supposed to have been down to the Law Library, and that they were calling for me, to come down there immediately! I told him that he could tell them that I was never going to be coming back down there to work ever again! He looked at me, then said that if I did not go to my assigned job, I know that he was going to have to write this up and that I was going to get into trouble, quite possible, put into the hole for at least 10 days or more? Then he said Smitty man don't make me do this to you! I then looked him dead in his eyes and told him that by the time that you have a hearing on your write up, I will be a free man! He immediately went and got on the phone, I am sure that he called the Wardens office and repeated that which I said to him, because when he came back, he said, man you can do as you damn well please! These are the direct orders from the warden himself! I then went back into my cell and started thinking about what it was, that I was going to do with the rest of my life after I got out of this hell hole! Even I had to admit that my future didn't look too bright from where I now stood! When I talked to my brother, he told me that my ex-wife was getting married to some older man that was living up here. (in Chicago) the house that we lived in was fixed back to perfection and was simply sold to another family while my wife and I were still yet locked up in the county jail! My wife and I were forced to look on as they took the belongings from out of our house and buried them in the city dump which was right next to the county jail! They sent me a letter notifying me of the fact that they were taking my car to the auto grave yard and putting it into the crusher, which is exactly what they did! Now they have illegally held me under arrest and in this prison for almost three years and now they are simply going to put me out on the streets with nothing in my pockets and no where to go! LIFE REALLY AIN'T FAIR! BUT WHO SAID THAT IT WOULD BE? As the week slowly drifted on by, I think that everybody kind of knew, that something was up with me, because, I didn't come out of my cell at all, except to shower and eat my meals! I didn't give a damn about anything or anybody at this point! All that I wanted was to be left the fuck alone because I now realized that not one single person in this place gives a flying fuck about nobody but themselves! Now that I have straightened out my business with those who violated me, everybody wanted to now be my friend! I only laughed at their attempts! As I knew, what even the Warden of this prison didn't know, which was, that I am out of here! Within the next now two days! As I went into my cell to once again think over my life, as a free man, it suddenly dawned on me, that I had one thousand dollars waiting on me, on the books! This was definitely going to be a real blessing, the GOOD LORD knows, that I am definitely going to need it, to get my life going! This kind of made me see things through a different perspective, because I now at least was going to be able to get myself a room, in a rooming house, which meant that I could get my life going once again, even though I did have to start all over from square #1. The next morning was Friday, and according to what that agent from the F.B.I. had said, this was supposed to be my very last day behind bars of any kind! I already knew that I can never believe what people of the law tell you especially when you are an inmate in a State ran institution, so I simply decided to just keep quiet and say absolutely nothing! When I got up to piss it was just a little after five o'clock in the morning, those inmates who worked on the outside of the prison details were being called to get ready to head toward their various assignments! Shortly after they were called those of us who were going to various assignments inside the prison were being called! Then after they were all called and were out of the way, they called those of us who were to do work inside of the actual area that we were now residing in, and this was supposed to have been everybody except myself and Scrap Iron, I still yet often wondered why was it that Scrap Iron never went on any kind of work details? But it really wasn't none of my business and it didn't reduce my time one way or the other! This particular Friday morning they were supposed to spray for bugs, which meant that every single inmate had to come out of their cells, whether they wanted to or not! We all had to come down to the middle of the prison where we could look at the State owned television! Just as they were finding the Good Morning America program on the T.V. we all heard them as they called for the inmate named James S. Smith Jr., prison number – EF309061 – report to The Wardens Office, with all bags packed! At that point Scrap Iron jumped up from his seat and said Smitty baby they are finally playing your tune! Why didn't you tell me that you were on your way out? Man, we could have tasted one of my ladies for your goodbye party? (drank whiskey) I told him, that I don't need any of your ladies, to realized that you are nothing but a bullshit motherfucker, and the further away from your black ass that I get, the better I will like it and the better off I will be! Then I told him that I wanted to tell you that I knew all the time that it was your mother/fucking ass that sent those four niggers after me in the first place, because just before I put the last one of them in the twilight zone he tricked on your stupid ass, begging me to please don't kill him! Your punk ass think that you really have your shit together, but I personally can make you this promise, and you can bet your last dime that I would have done this! Nigger I was going to KILL YOUR PUNK ASS! You had better thank your GOD, that he moved me back into the free world! Because within two weeks time I had already planned on taking your punk ass completely out of the game! I grabbed my personal belongings then I left, when I arrived at the Warden's office he directed me into the direction of the two armed sheriffs who had Leg Irons and Shackles in their hands, they place them on me, making sure that they were securely locked, then they double checked my identification card, making sure that I was, who I said I was, next they took me out to their waiting squad car, where they took me to the Senior Judge's privet chambers in downtown

59

Atlanta Georgia! Upon our arrival the Judge asked the two sheriffs, if they had brought all of my personal stuff with them, including the money that I had on the books, they looked at each other and said, they had forgotten to get the money from my account! The Senior Judge, immediately sent them back to the prison, telling them to learn how to do like I tell you to do! He told me to have a seat, Mr. Smith, You Have Been Through PURE HELL and I am this day, going to set you free! This you can be sure of! Just as soon as they come back in here, with the rest of your personal belongings! I didn't give a damn who saw me, the tears started rolling down my face as if somebody had stuck a hole in the dyke and the water started dripping, I looked toward heaven and said THANK YOU LORD! As soon as the two sheriff's returned, the Senior Judge told one of the officers, to show Mr. Smith to the bathroom and allow him to change his clothes, then show him his way back to this office, at which point, you two can leave, Mr. Smith, WILL NOT EVER, be going to prison with you again! Once you bring him back to this door your assignments are finished!

The Senior Judge was absolutely correct, because, when I gave it some thought, I actually felt as if I truly had Been To Hell! But through the grace of ALL MIGHTY GOD, I SOMEHOW MADE IT BACK TO TELL THIS STORY! The Senior Judge, informed me of the fact that he had granted me my Habeas Corpus Petition, and that I would be getting my court issued copy from this court informing me of this fact, through the United States Postal System! Within the next two months! Then he said, YOU ARE FREE TO GO. It was exactly two months precisely that I did receive my information in the mail, which told me that my conviction had been officially overturned! Once the Senior Judge issued his order, which overturned this illegal conviction, I then filed my Civil Action against The Arresting Detective, Clayton County Georgia and The State Of Georgia! Asking for $50 Million Dollars in Punitive and Compensatory Damages! I filed this civil action in the United States Federal District Court For The Northern District Of Georgia, Atlanta Circuit! Upon my submitting this civil action in the exact same court in which this illegal conviction was overturned, I felt somewhat, as if I was going to possibly get a fair hearing. Especially when the exact same judge that overturned this illegal conviction, for violations my constitutional rights, was the judge who was now hearing my submitted civil action, who is named; Richard C. Freeman, (Senior Judge) United States District Court For The Northern District Atlanta Circuit! However this judge not only ruled against my submitted Legal Brief Of

Law, he never allowed me the opportunity to come into his court to present the issues pertaining to this case at all! This judge simply issued an order of Summery Judgment in favor of the opposing party! This judge actually overturned my conviction, when he granted me the Habeas Corpus Petition, releasing me four years before my scheduled release date! Which automatically means that there was definitely some kind of Civil, Human And Or Constitutional Violation that took place pertaining to this case or else, the conviction could not have been overturned! Then this exact same judge simply kicked my case out of the court by granting the opposing party their requested Summery Judgment! The VIOLATIONS SEEMED TO NEVER END!

IN THE UNITED STATES DISTRICT COURT
FOR THE NORTHERN DISTRICT OF GEORGIA
ATLANTA DIVISION

JAMES SOLOMAN SMITH, JR.   :
                            :

   vs.   :   1:96-cv-2102-RCF

                                 :

R. T. SPIVEY and CLAYTON COUNTY,   :
GEORGIA
                                 :

O R D E R

This action is before the court on defendants' motion for summary judgment [#49-1] and

motion for an extension of time in which to file the pretrial order [#48-1], as well as numerous

motions filed by plaintiff [#35-1, #36-1, #39-1, #40-1, #51-1].

Background

As the result of a fire in his home in 1992, plaintiff was convicted of first-degree arson in the

Superior Court of Clayton County, Georgia and sentenced to seven years' imprisonment. Plaintiff

subsequently filed a habeas corpus petition in which he argued, inter alia, that he was denied the

assistance of appointed counsel on his initial appeal as of right. This court determined that plaintiff's

argument was meritorious and thus conditionally granted his petition for a writ of habeas corpus,

ordering his release from custody unless the State of Georgia allowed plaintiff to pursue his appeal

as of right with the assistance of appointed counsel. See Smith v. Lewis, No. 1:94-cv-1493-RCF

(N.D. Ga. Mar. 12, 1996). Shortly thereafter, plaintiff commenced this action, seeking $50,000,000

in compensatory and punitive damages from defendants Clayton County and R. T. Spivey, a former detective with the Clayton County Police Department. Defendants now move for summary judgment on plaintiff's claims. Plaintiff opposes the motion and has also filed a number of miscellaneous motions.

Discussion

A. Plaintiff's Motions

Plaintiff first asks the court to send him subpoenas for nine witnesses. The court previously denied a similar motion that plaintiff filed because he neither submitted sufficient funds to cover witness fees and expenses nor explained the reason for seeking to subpoena the witnesses at issue. See Order dated May 12, 1998, at 2. Plaintiff has once again not addressed the court's concerns, and his motion is therefore denied. In addition, the court denies plaintiff's motion to compel because he has not, as Fed. R. Civ. P. 37 and L.R. 37.1 of this court require, certified that he has conferred in good faith with opposing counsel regarding the discovery requests at issue before filing the motion.

Plaintiff has also filed a document titled "motion of intent to appeal all negative decisions issued to this plaintiff by this court." To the extent that this motion seeks the certification of an interlocutory appeal, it is denied because plaintiff has not demonstrated that he is entitled to such an appeal under 28 U.S.C. § 1292. Lastly, plaintiff's motion for appointment of counsel on appeal is denied because has not shown the existence of exceptional circumstances warranting the appointment of counsel on his behalf. See Wahl v. McIver, 773 F.2d 1169, 1174 (11th Cir. 1985).

B. Defendants' Summary Judgment Motion

Under Fed. R. Civ. P. 56, the court should grant a motion for summary judgment where "there is no genuine issue as to any material fact and . . . the moving party is entitled to judgment as a matter of law." The movant carries his or her burden by showing the court that there is "an absence

2

of evidence to support the nonmoving party's case." <u>Celotex Corp. v. Catrett</u>, 477 U.S. 317, 325 (1986). If the movant satisfies this burden, the burden shifts "to the non-moving party to demonstrate that there is indeed a material issue of fact that precludes summary judgment." <u>Clark v. Coats & Clark, Inc.</u>, 929 F.2d 604, 608 (11th Cir. 1991). The court, resolving all reasonable doubts in favor of the nonmovant, must determine "whether a fair-minded jury could return a verdict for the plaintiff on the evidence presented." <u>Anderson v. Liberty Lobby, Inc.</u>, 477 U.S. 242, 252 (1986).

Plaintiff brings this action, presumably pursuant to 42 U.S.C. § 1983, as the result of constitutional violations that allegedly occurred during the course of his arson prosecution. Specifically, plaintiff alleges: (1) that his Fourth Amendment rights were violated when Spivey entered and searched his home without a warrant and subsequently arrested him for arson; (2) that his due process rights were violated when proper pretrial procedures were not followed; (3) that his Sixth Amendment rights were violated when he was forced to appear for certain pretrial proceedings without counsel; (4) that his substantive due process rights were violated when the indictment originally brought against him was amended; (5) that his Sixth Amendment rights were violated when he was provided ineffective assistance of counsel; (6) that he was denied a fair trial because the state court trial judge was biased against him; (7) that his due process rights were violated when he was not provided with a copy of the criminal trial transcript; and (8) that his due process rights were violated when he was denied counsel to assist him with his appeal.

Defendants point out that they are entitled to summary judgment on the bulk of plaintiff's claims because neither Clayton County nor Spivey had any personal involvement in plaintiff's state court criminal proceedings. Plaintiff has introduced no evidence of his own in opposition to defendants' summary judgment motion, and he has accordingly not sustained his burden of

3

demonstrating a genuine issue of material fact as to whether the named defendants are responsible for the alleged constitutional violations surrounding his state court trial and appeal.

The court is thus left with plaintiff's Fourth Amendment claims regarding Spivey's conduct. Plaintiff first alleges that Spivey's entry into and search of his home were unconstitutional because Spivey had not first obtained a search warrant. This claim fails because, under the exigency exception to the Fourth Amendment's warrant requirement, a law enforcement official may enter a building in order to fight a fire therein and may remain there for a reasonable time in order to determine the fire's origin as well as whether the fire has truly been extinguished. See Michigan v. Tyler, 98 S. Ct. 1942, 1950 (1978). An official may also seize any evidence of the fire's origin that is discovered in connection with such an investigation. Id. Defendants have introduced unrebutted evidence that Spivey entered and searched plaintiff's home after the fire was extinguished in order to assist firefighters and investigators in determining the cause of the fire as well as to ascertain whether any "hot spots" existed that might later flare up. See Spivey Aff; Horton Aff. This course of action did not violate plaintiff's Fourth Amendment rights.

Plaintiff also claims that his arrest for arson violated the Fourth Amendment. "[A]n arrest made without probable cause violates the Fourth Amendment." Redd v. City of Enterprise, 140 F.3d 1378, 1382 (11th Cir. 1998). The standard for probable cause is an objective one, namely, "whether a reasonable man would have believed [probable cause existed] had he known all of the facts known by the officer." Rankin v. Evans, 133 F.3d 1425, 1433 (11th Cir. 1998) (internal citations and quotations omitted). Spivey states that plaintiff's arrest was predicated on evidence of accelerants found inside his home and inconsistent statements given by plaintiff and his wife following the fire. Spivey Aff., ¶¶ 9, 17. Plaintiff has not challenged this evidence through the introduction of any

4

evidence of his own. The court concludes that there was sufficient probable cause to support the issuance of a warrant for plaintiff's arrest, and Spivey is thus entitled to summary judgment on plaintiff's claims. Moreover, because no constitutional violation occurred, Clayton County is likewise entitled to summary judgment. See Rooney v. Watson, 101 F.3d 1378, 1381 (11th Cir. 1996) (affirming entry of summary judgment in favor of county where no underlying constitutional violation had been committed by county employee), cert. denied, 118 S. Ct. 412 (1997).

Conclusion

Accordingly, defendants' motion for summary judgment [#49-1] is GRANTED. Plaintiff's motions [#35-1, #36-1, #39-1, #40-1] are DENIED, with the exception of his motion for an extension of time [#51-1], which is GRANTED nunc pro tunc. Defendants' motion for an extension of time in which to file the pretrial order [#48-1] is DENIED as MOOT. The Clerk is DIRECTED to TERMINATE any remaining submissions, to ENTER JUDGMENT in favor of defendants, and to CLOSE this file.

SO ORDERED, this _2_ day of October, 1998.

for _____
RICHARD C. FREEMAN
SENIOR UNITED STATES DISTRICT JUDGE

Comes now James Soloman Smith Jr..

Who now submits the following pages, which will surely inform you, the skeptical reader, of the fact that every single word contained herein is the absolute truth! This truth, has been pledged to under penalty of perjury and if for any reason, the information contained herein was incorrect, I personally would at the very least, be standing before a Court Of Justice, answering to any stated lies which would be contained herein!

YET NOTHING HAS OCCURRED, SIMPLY BECAUSE, EVERY SINGLE WORD CONTAINED HEREIN, IS THE ABSOLUTE TRUTH TRUTH!

Sincerely,

James Soloman Smith Jr

The Author!

Thank you for using AOL GovernmentGuide Mail System

Message sent to the following recipients:

President Bush

Message text follows:

James Soloman Smith Jr.

April 2, 2003

[recipient address was inserted here]

Dear [recipient name was inserted here],

MR. PRESIDENT, I DO REALIZE THAT YOU ARE AN EXTREMELY BUSY PERSON AT THIS PARTICULAR TIME BUT SIR, AS ONE OF YOUR LOYAL REGISTERED VOTERS I WOULD LIKE TO ONCE AGAIN INFORM YOU OF HOW MY WIFE AND I, WERE ILLEGALLY ARRESTED FOR A CRIME THAT WE NOT ONLY DID NOT COMMIT, BUT, IT WAS FOUND OUT THAT WHAT WE WERE ARRESTED FOR, ACCORDING TO THE WRITTEN LAWS, WHICH ARE CURRENTLY ON THE LAW

BOOKS! WE NEVER BROKE ANY KIND OF LAW WHAT SO EVER! MR. PRESIDENT, THEY MADE ME FIGHT A JURY TRIAL WHICH LASTED FOR TWO WEEKS WITHOUT ANY KIND OF LEGAL REPRESENTATION! THEY USED A FRAUDULENT INDICTMENT AGAINST ME AND WHEN I POINTED OUT THAT THE INDICTMENT WAS A FRAUD, THE PRESIDING JUDGE LEFT THE COURTROOM CHECKED OUT WHAT I HAD INFORMED HIM OF, THEN WHEN HE RETURNED TO THE COURTROOM HE SIMPLY SPLIT THE CHARGING TERMS OF THE INDICTMENT IN HALF! FURTHER VIOLATING THE INDICTMENT, AS NO ONE CAN CHANGE OR ALTER THE TERMS OF AN INDICTMENT AFTER IT HAS BEEN RETURNED FROM THE GRAND JURY! SIR THE PRESIDING JUDGE SIMPLY RAILROADED ME INTO PRISON! FOR A CRIME IN WHICH NO LAW WAS EVER BROKEN! SIR, THESE VIOLATIONS WERE SO OBVIOUS, UNTIL WHEN I APPEALED THEM UP TO THE UNITED STATES FEDERAL DISTRICT COURT, THE SENIOR PRESIDING JUDGE OF SAID COURT, READ OF THE VIOLATIONS THEN IMMEDIATELY OVERTURNED THE CONVICTION BY GRANTING ME A HABEAS CORPUS PETITION! MR. PRESIDENT, I AM ONLY SENDING YOU A SMALL SAMPLE OF THE VIOLATIONS WHICH TOOK PLACE PERTAINING TO HOW MY WIFE AND I WERE TREATED BY THE SO CALLED JUSTICE SYSTEM IN THE STATE OF GEORGIA! SIR PEOPLE ARE BEING SENT TO PRISON DOWN IN THIS STATE ON A REGULAR BASIS, SIMPLY BECAUSE OF THE COLOR OF THEIR SKIN! AS RACISM STILL RUNS RAMPED DOWN IN THIS STATE!

Sincerely,
James S. Smith Jr.

Subj: Re: **VIOLATIONS OF MY CIVIL, HUMAN AND MY CONSTITUTIONAL RIGHTS**

Date: 4/2/3003 11:31:43 PM Central Standard Time

From: Autoresponder@WhiteHouse.GOV

To: SmJam117@aol.com

Sent from the Internet (Details)

Thank you for emailing President Bush. Your ideas and comments are very important to him.

For up-to-date information about the President and his policies, please check the White House web site at www.whitehouse.gov.

Unfortunately, because of the large volume of email received, the President cannot personally respond to each message. However, the White House staff considers and reports citizen ideas and concerns.

Again, thank you for your email. Your interest in the work of President Bush and his administration is appreciated.

Sincerely,

The White House Office of E-Correspondence

————————————

Please Note:

If the subject of your email was a request for a Presidential greeting, please not that all greeting requests must be submitted in writing to the following address:

The White House
Attn: Greetings Office
Room 39
Washington, D.C. 30502-0039

Please review the guidelines carefully before mailing your request to the White House. The guidelines are accessible at:

http://www.whitehouse.gov/greeting/

Received: from mail-s03.websys.aol.com ([64.12.180.167])
by WHITEHOUSE.GOV (PMDF V5.2-33 #41062)
with ESMTP id <01KU9SOQK1T49CCWFO@WHITEHOUSE.GOV> for
president@Whitehouse.GOV; Thu, 3 Apr 2003 00:26:08 EST
Received: from gov-s05.websys.aol.com (gov-s05.websys.aol.com [64.12.151.69])
by mail-s03.websys.aol.com (8.12.9/8.12.7) with SMTP id h32G50sPO12027 for
<president@whitehouse.gov>; Wed, 02 Apr 2003 11:-5:24 –0500 (EST)
Date: Wed, 02 Apr 2003 11:05:24 +0000 (%z)
From: "James Soloman Smith Jr." <SmJam117@aol.com>
Subject: VIOLATIONS OF MY CIVIL, HUMAN AND MY CONSTITUTIONAL RIGHTS
To: "the Honorable George W. Bush" <president@Whitehouse.GOV>
Message-id: <200304021605.h32G50sPO12027@mail-s03.websys.aol.com>
MIME-version: 1.0
X-Mailer: SMTP-Mailer
Content-type: text/plain; CHARSET=US-ASCII
Content-transfer-encoding: 7BIT

Subj: Re: **VIOLATIONS OF MY CIVIL, HUMAN AND MY CONSTITUTIONAL RIGHTS**

Date: 4/2/3003 10:31:49 PM Central Standard Time

From: SmJam117@aol.com

To: SmJam117@aol.com

Sent from the Internet (Details)

Thank you for using AOL GovenmentGuide Mail System

Message sent to the following recipients:

Rep. Hastert

Message text follows:

James Soloman Smith Jr.

April 2, 2003

[recipient address was inserted here]

Dear [recipient name was inserted here],

GREETINGS ONCE AGAIN, HONORED ELECTED OFFICIAL!

AS ONE OF THE PEOPLE THAT YOU ARE REPRESENTING, I WANT TO ASK YOU TO PLEASE TELL ME EXACTLY WHAT YOU INTENTIONS, PERTAINING TO THE VIOLATIONS WHICH I HAVE PRESENTED TO YOU! CONCERNING HOW MY WIFE AND I WERE ILLEGALLY ARRESTED FOR A CRIME THAT WE NOT ONLY

DID NOT COMMIT, BUT, IT WAS FOUND OUT THAT WHAT WE WERE ARRESTED FOR, ACCORDING TO THE LAWS WHICH ARE CURRENTLY ON THE LAW BOOKS! WE NEVER BROKE ANY KIND OF LAW WHAT SO EVER! THE ARRESTING OFFICER SEARCHED AND SEIZED ITEMS FROM MY HOUSE WITHOUT ANYTHING WHICH WOULD REMOTELY RESEMBLE A SEARCH WARRANT! HE ASSUMED THAT MY WIFE AND OR I SET OUR HOUSE ON FIRE AND ARRESTED THE BOTH OF US, WHILE WE CONSTANTLY TOLD HIM THAT WE WOULD NOT DO SUCH A THING! WHEN THIS CASE WAS BROUGHT INTO THE SUPERIOR COURT FOR THE STATE OF GEORGIA, THEY MADE ME FIGHT A JURY TRIAL WHICH LASTED FOR TWO WEEKS WITHOUT ANY KIND OF LEGAL REPRESENTATION! THE INDICTMENT WHICH WAS USED AGAINST ME WAS A FRAUDULENT INDICTMENT, AND WHEN I INFORMED THE PRESIDING JUDGE OF THIS FACT HE GOT UP AND LEFT THE COURTROOM CHECKED, THEN HE RETURNED TO THE COURTROOM AND SIMPLY SPLIT THE CHARGING TERMS OF THE INDICTMENT IN HALF! YET THE LAW SAYS THAT IT IS AGAINST THE CONSTITUTION FOR ANYONE TO CHANGE OR ALTER AN INDICTMENT AFTER IT HAS BEEN RETURNED FROM THE GRAND JURY! SIR, THE VIOLATIONS WERE SO SEVERE, UNTIL WHEN I APPEALED THEM UP TO THE UNITED STATES FEDERAL DISTRICT COURT, THE SENIOR JUDGE OF THAT COURT READ OF THE VIOLATIONS WHICH OCCURRED, THEN IMMEDIATELY OVERTURNED THE CONVICTION, BY GRANTING ME THE HABEAS CORPUS PETITION, WHICH I HAD REQUESTED IN MY BRIEF OF LAW! SIR, I ONCE AGAIN ASK YOU, AS MY ELECTED OFFICIAL, TO TELL ME WHAT ARE YOUR INTENTIONS, AS FAR AS HELPING MY WIFE AND I, GET THE CONSTITUTIONALLY GUARANTEED JUSTICE THAT WE ARE SUPPOSED TO BE GIVEN?

Sincerely,

James S. Smith Jr.

Subj: **GREETINGS MR. WYCLIFF, PLEASE TELL ME IF THIS WAS A FAST AND SPEEDY TRIAL**

Date: 4/3/2003 7:42:56 PM Central Standard Time

From: SmJam117

To: Dwycliff@tribune.com

GREETINGS MR. WYCLIFF MY NAME IS JAMES SOLOMAN SMITH JR., AND I HAVE RECENTLY READ YOUR SUBMITTED STORY IN BLACK VOICES! THE ONE IN WHICH YOU EXPRESSED THAT EVERY CITIZEN HAS THE CONSTITUTIONAL RIGHT TO A FAST AND SPEEDY TRIAL! SIR FAR BE IT FROM ME TO DISPUTE THAT WHICH YOU HAVE WRITTEN BUT, I FEEL IT MY DUTY TO INFORM YOU OF THE FACT THAT YOU ARE MAKING A SERIOUS MISTAKE! SIR YOU ARE DEAD WRONG IN YOUR STATEMENT THAT EVERY CITIZEN HAS GOTTEN OR WILL GET A FAST A ND SPEEDY TRIAL! SIR, I MAKE THIS ASSESSMENT FROM PURE FIRST HAND EXPERIENCE!

I AM SURE THAT YOU ARE NOT GOING TO EVEN RESPOND TO THIS TRANSMISSION, AS I PERSONALLY HAVE WRITTEN TO EVERY NEWS AGENCY KNOW TO THIS COUNTRY, TELLING THEM OF HOW MY FAMILY HAS BEEN ILLEGALLY ARRESTED, ILLEGALLY PROSECUTED AND I PERSONALLY WAS ILLEGALLY SENT TO PRISON, FOR A CRIME THAT I NOT ONLY DID NOT COMMIT, BUT, IT WAS SHOWN IN THE COURT ROOM THAT ACCORDING TO THE WRITTEN LAWS WHICH ARE CURRENTLY ON THE LAW BOOKS, NO CRIME WAS COMMITTED, NO LAW WAS EVER BROKEN! SIR AS FOR YOUR ASSESSMENT PERTAINING TO THE FAST AND SPEEDY TRIAL GOES! MY WIFE AND I WERE ARRESTED AND WE FILLED OUT THE NECESSARY FORMS FOR AN ATTORNEY TO BE APPOINTED TO OUR CASE! THIS NEVER HAPPENED, MY WIFE AND I WERE HELD IN THE CLAYTON COUNTY GEORGIA DETENTION

FACILITY FOR (52) FIFTY TWO DAYS BEFORE WE WERE TAKEN INTO ANY KIND OF A COURTROOM, AND WHEN WE WERE TAKEN INTO OUR FIRST COURT OF LAW, WE DID NOT HAVE ANY KIND OF REPRESENTATION!

ALL QUESTIONS THAT WERE ASKED OF OUR ACCUSERS WERE ASKED BY ME! NOT ONLY DID THIS OCCUR TO ME IN THIS COURTROOM, BUT WHEN WE WERE TAKEN INTO THE SUPERIOR COURT OF CLAYTON COUNTY GEORGIA MY WIFE WAS ASSIGNED THE SERVICES OF AN ATTORNEY, BUT THE PRESIDING JUDGE TOLD ME IN FRONT OF THE ENTIRE COURTROOM THAT UNDER NO CIRCUMSTANCES WAS HE GOING TO GIVE ME THE SERVICES OF AN ATTORNEY, FORCING ME INTO SELF REPRESENTATION, OF A JURY TRIAL THAT LASTED FOR TWO WEEKS! SIR I EVEN INFORMED THE PRESIDING JUDGE OF THE FACT THAT THE INDICTMENT WHICH HE WAS USING AGAINST ME WAS A FRAUDULENT INDICTMENT, I EVEN INFORMED HIM OF WHERE THE ERRORS WERE OBTAINED AND HOW THIS MADE THE INDICTMENT NOT A TRUE BILL AS INDICATED ON ITS FACE! THE JUDGE LEFT THE COURTROOM CHECKING AND FINDING OUT THAT WHAT I HAD TOLD HIM WAS TRUE, THEN WHEN HE RETURNED TO THE COURTROOM HE SIMPLY SPLIT THE CHARGING TERMS IN HALF, THIS WAS AFTER THE INDICTMENT HAD BEEN RETURNED FROM THE GRAND JURY! SIR I AM POSITIVE THAT YOU HAVE ALL KIND OF ACCESS TO AN ATTORNEY JUST IN CASE YOU ARE NOT FAMILIAR WITH COURTROOM PROCEDURES, SIR IF YOU CHECK, I KNOW THAT YOU WILL FIND OUT THAT NO ONE CAN ALTER AN INDICTMENT IN ANY MANNER WHAT SO EVER! ONCE IT HAS BEEN RETURNED FROM A GRAND JURY! SIR THE VIOLATIONS WERE SO SEVERE, UNTIL WHEN I APPEALED THESE VIOLATIONS UP TO THE UNITED STATES FEDERAL DISTRICT (COURT UNDER PRO-SE CONDITIONS) THE SENIOR JUDGE OF THAT COURT READ OF THE VIOLATIONS THAT OCCURRED, CHECKED THEM OUT TO MAKE SURE THAT WHAT I SAID WAS THE TRUTH THEN HE GRANTED ME A HABEAS CORPUS PETITION, RELEASING ME FROM ANY AND ALL FURTHER IMPRISONMENT! SIR LIKE I PREVIOUSLY STATED, I AM SURE THAT YOU MORE THAN LIKELY WILL NOT RESPOND TO THIS TRANSMISSION JUST AS SO MANY OTHER HAVE NOT

RESPONDED! BUT I HAVE MADE IT MY PERSONAL BUSINESS TO TELL EVERYONE THAT I CAN AND I HAVE EVERY INTENTION TO CONTINUE DOING THIS, FOR AS LONG AS IT TAKES ME TO FIND THE JUSTICE THAT I AM NOW SEEKING! SIR, IF YOU SHOULD HAVE ANY DESIRE WHAT SO EVER TO RESPOND TO THIS TRANSMISSION, IT JUST MIGHT BE TO LATE, BECAUSE THE POWERS THAT BE, ARE GOING TO CUT ME OFF OF THE INTERNET SIMPLY BECAUSE I KEEP FIGHTING FOR THE JUSTICE THAT I KNOW IN MY HEART THAT MY FAMILY WAS SURELY DENIED! THEY ARE TURNING OFF MY TELEPHONE ALSO! BUT THEY CANNOT STOP THE UNITED STATES POST OFFICE AND I WILL SURELY GO THERE! IF I HAVE TO CRAWL!
(IF YOU ARE INTERESTED MY CONTACT INFORMATION IS AS FOLLOWS)
JAMES SOLOMAN SMITH JR.

SIR I DO REALIZE THAT YOU DON'T HAVE ANY REASON WHAT SO EVER TO ACCEPT ANYTHING THAT I HAVE WRITTEN AS A FACT SIMPLY BECAUSE OF MY WRITTEN WORD! THEREFORE, I ISSUE YOU THIS LEGALLY BINDING STATEMENT!

"I JAMES SOLOMAN SMITH JR., DO SOLEMNLY SWEAR THAT EVERY STATEMENT ISSUED IN THIS DOCUMENT IS THE ABSOLUTE TRUTH, AND THAT I HAVE THE COURT DOCUMENTATION WHICH BACKS UP EVERYTHING THAT I HAVE WRITTEN HEREIN, I PLEDGE TO THIS TRUTH UNDER PENALTY OF PERJURY!!

Subj: RE**: Feedback Form Submission**

Date: 4/10/2003 2:46:07 PM Central Standard Time

From: info@ccr-ny.org

To: SmJam117@aol.com

Sent from the internet (Details)

Thank you for contacting CCR's general intake e-mail system. Please note that CCR litigates cases that we hope will benefit the lives of as many people as possible. Our focus is on the areas of government/police misconduct, racial justice, lesbian and gay rights, free speech, women's rights, public interest or international law. Regrettably, CCR does not have the capacity to handle most individual cases. If you are facing a deadline, we urge you to contact another law firm in the interim.

If you believe your case would be of interest to the CCR and would like it to be reviewed by out Intake Committee, we ask you to submit a brief written statement to us at The Center for Constitutional Rights, 666 Broadway, 7th Floor, New York, NY 10012, Attention: General

Intake. Please do not send us original documents, as we may not be able to return them. Upon review of your case, which may take some time, we will make every effort to respond to you in writing. If CCR is not able to assist you directly, we will try to include references to an attorney and/or organization that may be able to provide you with the appropriate assistance. However, in some cases, we may not be able to respond to you or provide you with referrals. We wish you the best in finding the assistance you seek.

Country: USA

User Name: James S. Smith Jr.

Address:

User Email:

City/Town:

State:

Referred By: Word of mouth

Zip/Postal Code:

Phone:————————-NONE——————

Fax: ——————-NONE——————

Prior Visits: 4-6 times

Comments: GREETINGS, MY NAME IS JAMES SOLOMAN SMITH JR. AND AS I HAVE BEEN READING OVER YOU WEB-SITE, I STRONGLY FEEL THAT YOU ARE THE PEOPLE THAT I HAVE BEEN SEARCHING FOR! MY PRAYERS NOW ARE THAT YOU ARE WILLING TO ACCEPT ME AS ONE OF THE PEOPLE THAT YOU ARE WILLING TO ASSIST! MY WIFE AND I WERE ARRESTED FOR A CRIME THAT WE NOT ONLY DID NOT COMMIT, BUT IT WAS FOUND OUT THAT WHAT WE WERE ARRESTED FOR ACCORDING TO THE WRITTEN LAWS WHICH ARE CURRENTLY ON THE LAW BOOKS, WE NEVER BROKE ANY KIND OF LAW WHAT SO EVER! WE WERE ARRESTED FOR SETTING OUR OWN HOUSE ON FIRE, THE ONE IN WHICH WE RESIDED, ALONG WITH OUR FOUR CHILDREN! THE ARRESTING OFFICER SIMPLY ASSUMED THAT MY WIFE AND I SET OUR HOUSE ON FIRE, THEN PLACED US BOTH UNDER ARREST, HE DID NOT HAVE ONE SINGLE WITNESS, NO PROOF, AND NOT A SINGLE THREAD OF EVIDENCE,

WHICH COULD, OR WOULD POINT THE FINGER OF GUILT, AT EITHER MY WIFE
OR I! IN FACT, MY WIFE

AND I CONSTANTLY TOLD THE ARRESTING OFFICER, THAT HE WAS MAKING A SERIOUS MISTAKE, AS WE WOULD NOT DO SUCH A THING TO OUR HOUSE! HE SIMPLY IGNORED EVERYTHING THAT WE WERE SAYING! AFTER WE WERE PUT INTO THE COUNTY JAIL, WE WERE NOT TAKEN INTO ANY KIND OF A COURT ROOM FOR (52) FIFTY-TWO DAYS! THEN, WHEN WE WERE TAKEN INTO THE FIRST COURT OF LAW, WE DID NOT HAVE ANY KIND OF LEGAL REPRESENTATION! ALL QUESTIONS THAT WERE ASKED OF OUR ACCUSERS, WERE ASKED BY ME! YET, WE BOTH SUBMITTED THE NECESSARY PAPERS THAT SHOULD HAVE HAD AN ATTORNEY ASSIGNED TO REPRESENT US! ALSO, THE ONLY PEOPLE THAT WERE THERE TO TESTIFY AGAINST MY WIFE AND I, WERE THE ARRESTING OFFICER AND THE FIRE MARSHALL, OF WHICH NEITHER WAS ANYWHERE NEAR OUR HOUSE UNTIL AFTER THE FACT! THEREFORE, THEIR TESTIMONY SHOULD HAVE BEEN INADMISSIBLE IN ANY COURT OF LAW! WHEN WE WERE TAKEN BACK TO THE COUNTY JAIL THE ARRESTING OFFICER SENT TWO UNDERCOVER INFORMANTS INTO THE JAIL AREA AND THE CELL THAT I WAS BEING HELD IN, WITH ORDERS TO GATHER SOME KIND OF INCRIMINATING INFORMATION AGAINST ME! THEN, WHEN THEY WERE NOT ABLE TO GET ME TO SAY ANYTHING INCRIMINATING THEY SIMPLY TOLD LIES TO THE ARRESTING OFFICER, WHO IN TURN WENT TO THE GRAND JURY AND TOLD THEM THE LIES, WHICH THE GRAND JURY USED AND ISSUED A SECOND CHARGE AGAINST ME! WHICH WAS TOTALLY BASED ON THE LIES OF TWO ALREADY CONVICTED FELONS! IT SHOULD BE NOTED THAT I WAS NEVER GIVEN A BOND OF ANY KIND, THEREFORE I WAS LOCKED IN THE COUNTRY JAIL FOR MORE THAN SIX MONTHS BEFORE THIS CASE WAS BROUGHT INTO THE SUPERIOR COURT! THE INDICTMENT WHICH WAS ISSUED TO ME, STATED THAT I HAD OBTAINED A SECOND CHARGE WHILE I WAS STILL YET AWAITING TRIAL! HOWEVER, I WAS NEVER INFORMED OF THE FACT THAT I HAD RECEIVED A NEW CHARGE! I WAS NEVER FINGER

PRINTED PERTAINING TO THIS NEW CHARGE! I WAS NEVER ISSUED A COPY OF THIS NEW CHARGE! I NEVER EVEN HEARD OF THIS NEW CHARGE UNTIL TWO DAYS BEFORE I WAS TAKEN INTO THE SUPERIOR COURT FOR THE ACTUAL TRIAL! WHEN MY WIFE AND I WERE TAKEN INTO THE SUPERIOR COURT FOR THE TRIAL TO BEGIN, THE PRESIDING JUDGE ASSIGNED MY WIFE THE SERVICES OF AN ATTORNEY TO REPRESENT HER, THEN TOLD THE ENTIRE COURT THAT UNDER NO CIRCUMSTANCES WAS HE GOING TO ASSIGN ME THE SERVICES OF AN ATTORNEY! THEREBY FORCING ME INTO SELF REPRESENTATION! I WAS FORCED TO PICK OUT A JURY OF MY PEERS! I WAS FORCED TO ASK THOSE THAT I PICKED OVER QUESTIONS! I WAS FORCED TO DO EVERYTHING THAT AN ATTORNEY WOULD NORMALLY DO! IT SHOULD BE NOTED THAT THE EXTENT OF MY FORMAL EDUCATION, IS THAT I AM A HIGH SCHOOL GRADUATE! I HAVE NEVER WENT OT ANY KIND OF A LAW SCHOOL! AFTER THE PRESIDING JUDGE READ THE CHARGES OFF HE TOLD ME THAT ONCE THE GRAND JURY HAS ISSUED CHARGES AGAINST A PERSON THAT PERSON MUST ANSWER THOSE CHARGES, THOSE CHARGES CANNOT BE ALTERED IN ANY MANNER WHAT SO EVER, NOT BY THIS COURT, NOT BY THE DISTRICT ATTORNEY AND CERTAINLY NOT BY YOU MR. SMITH, THIS COURT THEREFORE WANTS TO KNOW HOW DO YOU INTEND TO PLEA TO THESE CHARGES THAT HAVE BEEN PRESENTED AGAINST YOU? AT THIS POINT I INFORMED THE PRESIDING JUDGE OF THE FACT THAT THE INDICTMENT WHICH WAS NOW BEING PRESENTED AGAINST ME WAS A FRAUDULENT INDICTMENT, AND NOT A TRUE

BILL

AS IS WRITTEN ON ITS FACE! I THEN EXPLAINED TO THE PRESIDING JUDGE OF THE FACT THAT I HAVE NEVER HEARD OF THE SECOND CHARGE WHICH WAS PRESENTED ON THE INDICTMENT, THAT I HAD NEVER BEEN FINGER PRINTED, THAT I HAVE NEVER HAD MY MIRANDA RIGHTS READ TO ME, PERTAINING TO THIS SECOND CHARGE, THAT I HAD NEVER BEEN INFORMED OF THIS CHARGE UNTIL I READ ABOUT IT WHEN I OBTAINED A COPY OF MY INDICTMENT! THE PRESIDING JUDGE GOT UP AND IMMEDIATELY LEFT THE COURTROOM, THEN WHEN HIS HONOR RETURNED TO THE COURTROOM HE SIMPLY SPLIT THE INDICTMENT IN HALF! THIS WAS DEFINITELY MUCH AFTER THE GRAND JURY HAD HANDED DOWN THIS INDICTMENT! (THIS ALONE VIOLATES THE GRAND JURY CLAUSE TO THE CONSTITUTION-5TH.AMENDMENT)! THERE IS SO VERY MUCH THAT I WOULD LIKE TO PRESENT TO YOU AND YOUR ORGANIZATION, BUT I DARE NOT PUT DOWN TOO MUCH MORE, AS THE FEAR THAT I NOW SUFFER WITH! THE POWERS THAT BE HAVE HAD MY PHONE CUT OFF! AND IN THE VERY NEAR FUTURE I AM GUESSING THAT THIS COMPUTER WILL BE SHUT OFF! HOWEVER THIS IS MY CONTACT INFORMATION:

JAMES SOLOMAN SMITH JR.

I solemnly swear that every single word contained herein is the absolute truth, I pledge to this truth under penalty of perjury!

Handled by: Form mailer http://www.ccr-ny.org/,2003

Subj: Re: **VIOLATIONS OF MY CIVIL, HUMAN AND MY CONSTITUTIONAL RIGHTS**

Date: 4/11/3003 3:45:53 PM Central Standard Time

From: SmJam117@aol.com

To: SmJam117@aol.com

Sent from the Internet (Details)

Thank you for using AOL GovernmentGuide Mail System

Message sent to the following recipients:

Atlanta Journal-Constitution

Jonesboro New Daily

Macon Telegraph

WSB-TV 2

WXIA (NBC-11)

Message text follows:

James Soloman Smith Jr.

April 11, 2003

[recipient address was inserted here]

Dear [recipient name was inserted here],

GREETINGS, MY NAME IS JAMES SOLOMAN SMITH JR.,

I USED TO LIVE IN CLAYTON COUNTY GEORGIA, UNTIL MY WIFE AND I WERE ILLEGALLY ARRESTED, ILLEGALLY PROSECUTED AND I PERSONALLY WAS ILLEGALLY SENT TO PRISON BY A RACIST POLICE OFFICER ON THE CLAYTON GEORGIA POLICE DEPARTMENT, NAMED DETECTIVE R.T. SPIVEY! THIS MAN ARRESTED MY WIFE AND I SIMPLY BECAUSE OF THE COLOR OF OUR SKIN! AS HE ARRESTED THE TWO OF US FOR A CRIME THAT WE NOT ONLY DID NOT COMMIT BUT IT WAS DISCOVERED THAT ACCORDING TO THE WRITTEN LAWS WHICH ARE CURRENTLY ON THE LAW BOOKS, NO LAW WAS EVER BROKEN BY ANYONE! YET I WAS FORCED TO FIGHT A JURY TRIAL WITHOUT ANYTHING WHICH COULD NOR WOULD REMOTELY RESEMBLE AN ATTORNEY! A TRIAL WHICH LASTED FOR TWO WEEKS! THE ARRESTING DETECTIVE CAME TO OUR HOUSE APPROXIMATELY TWO HOURS AFTER THE FIRE WHICH OCCURRED TO OUR HOUSE HAD BEEN TOTALLY EXTINGUISHED, HE GOT OUT OF HIS CAR! WALKED RIGHT PAST MY WIFE AND I, WENT UP AND TALKED WITH THE FIRE MARSHALL, FOR A FEW MOMENTS THEN THE TWO OF THEM WENT DIRECTLY INTO OUR HOUSE! MY WIFE AND I STOOD IN THE FRONT YARD AND LOOKED ON IN COMPLETE ASTONISHMENT, AS WE SAW THE FIRE MARSHALL AND THE ARRESTING DETECTIVE, AS THEY WORKED TOGETHER, AS IF THEY WERE A TEAM! THE FIRE MARSHALL PULLED THE CARPET FROM THE FLOOR, WHILE THE DETECTIVE TOOK WHAT APPEARED TO BA A PAIR OF SHEERS AND CUT LARGE HOLES INTO OUR PROFESSIONALLY INSTALLED CARPET, THEY WENT THROUGH OUT THE HOUSE DOING THIS, THEN MY WIFE AND I CONTINUED TO LOOK ON, AS THEY FINISHED DOING THIS TO OUR CARPET! WE CONTINUED LOOKING ON AS THEY WENT INTO OUR LIVING ROOM, WHERE WE OBSERVED THEM AS THEY PROCEEDED TO CUT LARGE HOLES INTO THE FURNITURE IN THERE! THEY ASSISTED EACH OTHER AS THEY CUT HOLES INTO THE SOFA, THEN THE LOVE SEAT, FINALLY, THEY WENT INTO THE DINING ROOM, WHERE WE CONTINUED TO LOOK ON, AS THEY PROCEEDED TO CUT HOLES INTO THE CUSHIONS OF THE CHAIRS THAT WERE AROUND OUR DINING ROOM TABLE! THIS WAS DONE TO OUR HOUSE WITHOUT ANYONE HAVING A WARRANT OF

ANY KIND WHAT SO EVER! HAVING COMPLETED DOING THIS TO THE INTERIOR OF OUR HOUSE, THE DETECTIVE CAME OUT, WALKED UP TO MY WIFE AND I THEN SAID, "DO EITHER OF YOU TWO KNOW HOW THIS FIRE GOT STARTED?" MY WIFE AND I BOTH INFORMED THE

ARRESTING DETECTIVE OF THE FACT THAT WE DID NOT KNOW HOW THE FIRE HAD BEEN STARTED! HE THEN SAID, "SINCE THE TWO OF YOU DON'T KNOW HOW THE FIRE GOT STARTED AND I DON'T KNOW HOW THE FIRE GOT STARTED I AM NOW PLACING THE TWO OF YOU UNDER ARREST AND I AM CHARGING BOTH OF YOU WITH ARSON IN THE FIRST DEGREE!

Sincerely,

James S. Smith Jr.

Subj: **ARE YOU INTERESTED IN HEARING THIS TRUE STORY?**

Date: 4/1/2003 12:40;50 PM Central Standard Time

From: Date: 4/1/2003 12:40;50 PM Central Standard Time

From: SmJam117

To: editor@thesmokinggun.com

GREETINGS MY NAME IS JAMES SOLOMAN SMITH JR., THE REASON THAT I AM CORRESPONDING TO YOUR ORGANIZATION IS TO FIND OUT IF YOU ARE INTERESTED IN HEARING ABOUT HOW MY WIFE AND I WERE ILLEGALLY ARRESTED FOR A CRIME THAT WE NOT ONLY DID NOT COMMIT, BUT IT WAS FOUND OUT THAT WHAT WE WERE ARRESTED FOR, ACCORDING TO THE WRITTEN LAWS WHICH ARE CURRENTLY ON THE LAW BOOKS, WE NEVER BROKE THE LAW IN ANY MANNER WHAT SO EVER! YET, WE WERE PUT INTO THE COUNTY JAIL, AND WERE NOT ALLOWED TO GO IN FRONT OF ANY KIND OF A JUDGE OR MAGISTRATE FOR (52) FIFTY TWO DAYS! WHEN WE WERE TAKEN INTO THE SUPERIOR COURT FOR THE ACTUAL TRIAL MY WIFE WAS GIVEN AN ATTORNEY TO REPRESENT HER WHILE I WAS FORCED TO FIGHT A JURY TRIAL WHICH LASTED FOR TWO WEEKS WITHOUT ANY KIND OF REPRESENTATION! THERE ARE MANY MORE VIOLATIONS WHICH OCCURRED PERTAINING TO THIS CASE, THE VIOLATIONS WERE SO SEVERE UNTIL WHEN I APPEALED THESE VIOLATIONS UP TO THE UNITED STATES FEDERAL DISTRICT COURT (ALL BY MYSELF) THE SENIOR JUDGE OVERTURNED THE CONVICTION AND RELEASED ME FROM ANY FURTHER IMPRISONMENT, BY GRANTING ME THE HABEAS CORPUS PETITION!

I AM MORE THAN WILLING TO INFORM YOU OF ALL THE VIOLATIONS THAT TOOK PLACE PERTAINING TO THIS CASE! ALL THAT YOU HAVE TO DO IS TO GET INTO CONTACT WITH ME! AS I HAVE EVERY COURT CASE DOCUMENT NUMBER SO THAT YOU CAN CHECK AND MAKE SURE THAT WHAT I AM

WILLING TO PRESENT TO YOU IS AUTHENTIC AND THE TRUTH! I ALSO HAVE
IN MY POSSESSION THE ACTUAL REPLIES FROM EVERY COURT THAT I
APPEALED THIS CASE TO!
IF YOU ARE INTERESTED CONTACT ME IN THE FOLLOWING MANNER!
JAMES SOLOMAN SMITH JR.

Sunday, August 10, 2003 America Online: SmJam117

Subj: RE: **Feedback Form Submission**

Date: 4/10/2003 2:46:07 PM Central Standard Time

From: info@ccr-ny.org

To: SmJam117@aol.com

Sent from the Internet (Details)

Thank you for contacting CCR's general intake e-mail system. Please note that CCR litigates cases that we hope will benefit the lives of as many people as possible. Our focus is on the areas of government/police misconduct, racial justice, lesbian and gay rights, free speech, women's rights, public interest or international law. Regrettably, CCR does not have the capacity to handle most individual cases. If you are facing a deadline, we urge you to contact another law firm in the interim.

If you believe your case would be of interest to the CCR and would like it to be reviewed by out Intake Committee, we ask you to submit a brief written statement to us at The Center for Constitutional Rights, 666 Broadway, 7th Floor, New York, NY 10012, Attention: General Intake. Please do not send us original documents, as we may not be able to return them. Upon review of your case, which may take some time, we will make every effort to respond to you in writing. If CCR is not able to assist you directly, we will try to include references to an attorney and/or organization that may be able to provide you with the appropriate assistance. However, in some cases, we may not be able to respond to you or provide you with referrals. We wish you the best in finding the assistance you seek.

Country: USA

User Name: James S. Smith Jr.

Address:

User Email:

City/Town:

State:

Referred By: Word of mouth

Zip/Postal Code:

Phone:————————-NONE———————

Fax: ——————————-NONE——————

Prior Visits: 4-6 times

Comments: GREETINGS, MY NAME IS JAMES SOLOMAN SMITH JR. AND AS I HAVE BEEN

READING OVER YOU WEB-SITE, I STRONGLY FEEL THAT YOU ARE THE PEOPLE THAT I

HAVE BEEN SEARCHING FOR! MY PRAYERS NOW ARE THAT YOU ARE WILLING TO ACCEPT

ME AS ONE OF THE PEOPLE THAT YOU ARE WILLING TO ASSIST!

MY WIFE AND I WERE ARRESTED FOR A CRIME THAT WE NOT ONLY DID NOT COMMIT, BUT IT WAS FOUND OUT THAT WHAT WE WERE ARRESTED FOR ACCORDING TO THE WRITTEN LAWS WHICH ARE CURRENTLY ON THE LAW BOOKS, WE NEVER BROKE ANY KIND OF LAW WHAT SO EVER! WE WERE ARRESTED FOR SETTING

OUR OWN HOUSE ON FIRE, THE ONE IN WHICH WE RESIDED, ALONG WITH OUR FOUR CHILDREN! THE ARRESTING OFFICER SIMPLY ASSUMED THAT MY WIFE AND I SET OUR HOUSE ON FIRE, THEN PLACED US BOTH UNDER ARREST, HE DID NOT HAVE ONE SINGLE WITNESS, NO PROOF, AND NOT A SINGLE THREAD OF EVIDENCE, WHICH COULD, OR WOULD POINT THE FINGER OF GUILT, AT EITHER MY WIFE OR I! IN FACT, MY WIFE

AND I CONSTANTLY TOLD THE ARRESTING OFFICER, THAT HE WAS MAKING A SERIOUS MISTAKE, AS WE WOULD NOT DO SUCH A THING TO OUR HOUSE! HE SIMPLY IGNORED EVERYTHING THAT WE WERE SAYING! AFTER WE WERE PUT INTO THE COUNTY JAIL, WE WERE NOT TAKEN INTO ANY KIND OF A COURT ROOM FOR (52) FIFTY-TWO DAYS! THEN, WHEN WE WERE TAKEN INTO THE FIRST COURT OF LAW, WE DID NOT HAVE ANY KIND OF LEGAL REPRESENTATION! ALL QUESTIONS THAT WERE ASKED OF OUR ACCUSERS, WERE ASKED BY ME! YET, WE BOTH SUBMITTED THE NECESSARY PAPERS THAT SHOULD HAVE HAD AN ATTORNEY ASSIGNED TO REPRESENT US! ALSO, THE ONLY PEOPLE THAT WERE THERE TO TESTIFY AGAINST MY WIFE AND I, WERE THE ARRESTING OFFICER AND THE FIRE MARSHALL, OF WHICH NEITHER WAS ANYWHERE NEAR OUR HOUSE UNTIL AFTER THE FACT! THEREFORE, THEIR TESTIMONY SHOULD HAVE BEEN INADMISSIBLE IN ANY COURT OF LAW! WHEN WE WERE TAKEN BACK TO THE COUNTY JAIL THE ARRESTING OFFICER SENT TWO UNDERCOVER INFORMANTS INTO THE JAIL AREA AND THE CELL THAT I WAS BEING HELD IN, WITH ORDERS TO GATHER SOME KIND OF INCRIMINATING INFORMATION AGAINST ME! THEN, WHEN THEY WERE NOT ABLE TO GET ME TO SAY ANYTHING INCRIMINATING THEY SIMPLY TOLD LIES TO THE ARRESTING OFFICER, WHO IN TURN WENT TO THE GRAND JURY AND TOLD THEM THE LIES, WHICH THE GRAND JURY USED AND ISSUED A SECOND CHARGE AGAINST ME! WHICH WAS TOTALLY BASED ON THE LIES OF TWO ALREADY CONVICTED FELONS! IT SHOULD BE NOTED THAT I WAS NEVER GIVEN A BOND OF ANY KIND, THEREFORE I WAS LOCKED IN THE COUNTRY JAIL FOR MORE THAN SIX MONTHS BEFORE THIS CASE WAS BROUGHT INTO THE SUPERIOR COURT! THE INDICTMENT WHICH WAS ISSUED TO ME, STATED THAT I HAD OBTAINED A SECOND CHARGE WHILE I WAS STILL YET AWAITING TRIAL! HOWEVER, I WAS NEVER INFORMED OF THE FACT THAT I HAD RECEIVED A NEW CHARGE! I WAS NEVER FINGER

PRINTED PERTAINING TO THIS NEW CHARGE! I WAS NEVER ISSUED A COPY OF THIS NEW CHARGE! I NEVER EVEN HEARD OF THIS NEW CHARGE UNTIL TWO DAYS BEFORE I WAS TAKEN INTO THE SUPERIOR COURT FOR THE ACTUAL TRIAL! WHEN MY WIFE AND I WERE TAKEN INTO THE SUPERIOR COURT FOR THE TRIAL TO BEGIN, THE PRESIDING JUDGE ASSIGNED MY WIFE THE SERVICES OF AN ATTORNEY TO REPRESENT HER, THEN TOLD THE ENTIRE COURT THAT UNDER NO CIRCUMSTANCES WAS HE GOING TO ASSIGN ME THE SERVICES OF AN ATTORNEY! THEREBY FORCING ME INTO SELF REPRESENTATION! I WAS FORCED TO PICK OUT A JURY OF MY PEERS! I WAS FORCED TO ASK THOSE THAT I PICKED OVER QUESTIONS! I WAS FORCED TO DO EVERYTHING THAT AN ATTORNEY WOULD NORMALLY DO! IT SHOULD BE NOTED THAT THE EXTENT OF MY FORMAL EDUCATION, IS THAT I AM A HIGH SCHOOL GRADUATE! I HAVE NEVER WENT OT ANY KIND OF A LAW SCHOOL!

AFTER THE PRESIDING JUDGE READ THE CHARGES OFF HE TOLD ME THAT ONCE THE GRAND JURY HAS ISSUED CHARGES AGAINST A PERSON THAT PERSON MUST ANSWER THOSE CHARGES, THOSE CHARGES CANNOT BE ALTERED IN ANY MANNER WHAT SO EVER, NOT BY THIS COURT, NOT BY THE DISTRICT ATTORNEY AND CERTAINLY NOT BY YOU MR. SMITH, THIS COURT THEREFORE WANTS TO KNOW HOW DO YOU INTEND TO PLEA TO THESE CHARGES THAT HAVE BEEN PRESENTED AGAINST YOU? AT THIS POINT I INFORMED THE PRESIDING JUDGE OF THE FACT THAT THE INDICTMENT WHICH WAS NOW BEING PRESENTED AGAINST ME WAS A FRAUDULENT INDICTMENT, AND NOT A TRUE

BILL

AS IS WRITTEN ON ITS FACE! I THEN EXPLAINED TO THE PRESIDING JUDGE OF THE FACT THAT I HAVE NEVER HEARD OF THE SECOND CHARGE WHICH WAS PRESENTED ON THE INDICTMENT, THAT I HAD NEVER BEEN FINGER PRINTED, THAT I HAVE NEVER HAD MY MIRANDA RIGHTS READ TO ME, PERTAINING TO THIS SECOND CHARGE, THAT I HAD NEVER BEEN INFORMED OF THIS CHARGE UNTIL I READ ABOUT IT WHEN I OBTAINED A COPY OF MY INDICTMENT! THE PRESIDING JUDGE GOT UP AND IMMEDIATELY LEFT THE COURTROOM, THEN WHEN HIS HONOR RETURNED TO THE COURTROOM HE SIMPLY SPLIT THE INDICTMENT IN HALF! THIS WAS DEFINITELY MUCH AFTER THE GRAND JURY HAD HANDED DOWN THIS INDICTMENT! (THIS ALONE VIOLATES THE GRAND JURY CLAUSE TO THE CONSTITUTION-5TH.AMENDMENT)!

THERE IS SO VERY MUCH THAT I WOULD LIKE TO PRESENT TO YOU AND YOUR ORGANIZATION, BUT I DARE NOT PUT DOWN TOO MUCH MORE, AS THE FEAR THAT I NOW SUFFER WITH! THE POWERS THAT BE HAVE HAD MY PHONE CUT OFF! AND IN THE VERY NEAR FUTURE I AM GUESSING THAT THIS COMPUTER WILL BE SHUT OFF!

HOWEVER THIS IS MY CONTACT INFORMATION:

JAMES SOLOMAN SMITH JR.

I solemnly swear that every single word contained herein is the absolute truth, I pledge to this truth under penalty of perjury!

Handled by: Form mailer http://www.ccr-ny.org/,2003

Subj: RE: **Your recent message.**

Date: 4/2/2003 10:45:12 AM Central Standard Time

From: il14ima.pub@mail.house.gov

To: smjam17@aol.com

Sent from the Internet (Details)

Thank you very much for contacting my office about an issue that I know concerns you greatly. Please know that I have acknowledged and registered your opinion, and greatly appreciate hearing your views. At this time, I am only able to respond to residents of the 14th Congressional District of Illinois. If you included your name, address and zip code in your message, thank you. If not, please resend your message.

Thank you once again. Your comments are an integral part of the political process. Without them, I would not be able to make the decisions that affect our community and our nation.

Speaker J. Dennis Hastert

2369 Rayburn House Office Building

Washington, DC 20515

(202) 225-2976

Sunday, August 10, 2003 America Online: SmJam117

ABOUT THE AUTHOR

It should be noted about this author that he NEVER wanted to fight the powers that be, in any shape form or fashion, this fight was thrust upon this author, when he and his wife were ILLEGALLY ARRESTED FOR NO REASON WHAT SO EVER! It must be further noted that the author of this book, has NEVER BEEN INTO ANY KIND OF LEGAL TRAINING FACILITY OF ANY KIND WHAT SO EVER, BUT, HIS PARENTS HAD ALWAYS TAUGHT HIM HOW TO (FAST AND PRAY) TO THE GOD OF HIS UNDERSTANDING, ASKING HIM FOR HIS DIVINE INTERVENTION, IN SITUATIONS THAT WERE TOO LARGE FOR HIM TO ACCEPT OR UNDERSTAND AND HE (GOD) WILL HEAR YOUR PRAYERS! WHICH IS EXACTLY WHAT OCCURRED PERTAINING TO THE STUDYING OF THE VARIOUS LAWS AS THEY PERTAINED TO THIS CASE! THIS AUTHOR TAKES ABSOLUTELY NO CREDIT FOR WINNING HIS RELEASE FROM PRISON, WITHOUT ANY KIND OF ASSISTANCE, FROM ANY KIND OF A HUMAN, LEGAL REPRESENTATIVE! SIMPLY BECAUSE, HE CALLED ON THE VERY TOP ATTORNEY EVER KNOWN TO MANKIND, WHEN HE CALLED ON HIS ATTORNEY NAMED GOD ALL MIGHTY! THE ONE THAT HAS NEVER LOST ONE SINGLE CASE, EVER!

(AND NEVER, EVER, WILL)